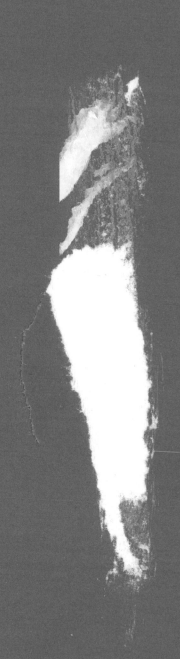

THE Dublin Marathon

Irish runners Brian Maher (23), Sean Hehir (2) and Colm Rooney (422) in the 2013 Dublin Marathon.

THE Dublin Marathon

Celebrating 40 Years

Sean McGoldrick

THE O'BRIEN PRESS
DUBLIN

First published 2019 by The O'Brien Press Ltd,
12 Terenure Road East, Rathgar,
Dublin 6, D06 HD27, Ireland.
Tel: +353 1 4923333; Fax: +353 1 4922777
E-mail: books@obrien.ie
Website: www.obrien.ie
The O'Brien Press is a member of Publishing Ireland.

ISBN: 978-1-78849-136-5

10 9 8 7 6 5 4 3 2 1
23 22 21 20 19

Printed and bound in Poland by Białostockie Zakłady Graficzne S.A.
The paper in this book is produced using pulp from managed forests.

Published in:

DUBLIN
UNESCO
City of Literature

Dedication:

For Pat, Donagh, Ronan and Johnny, who crossed the finish line too soon.

Contents

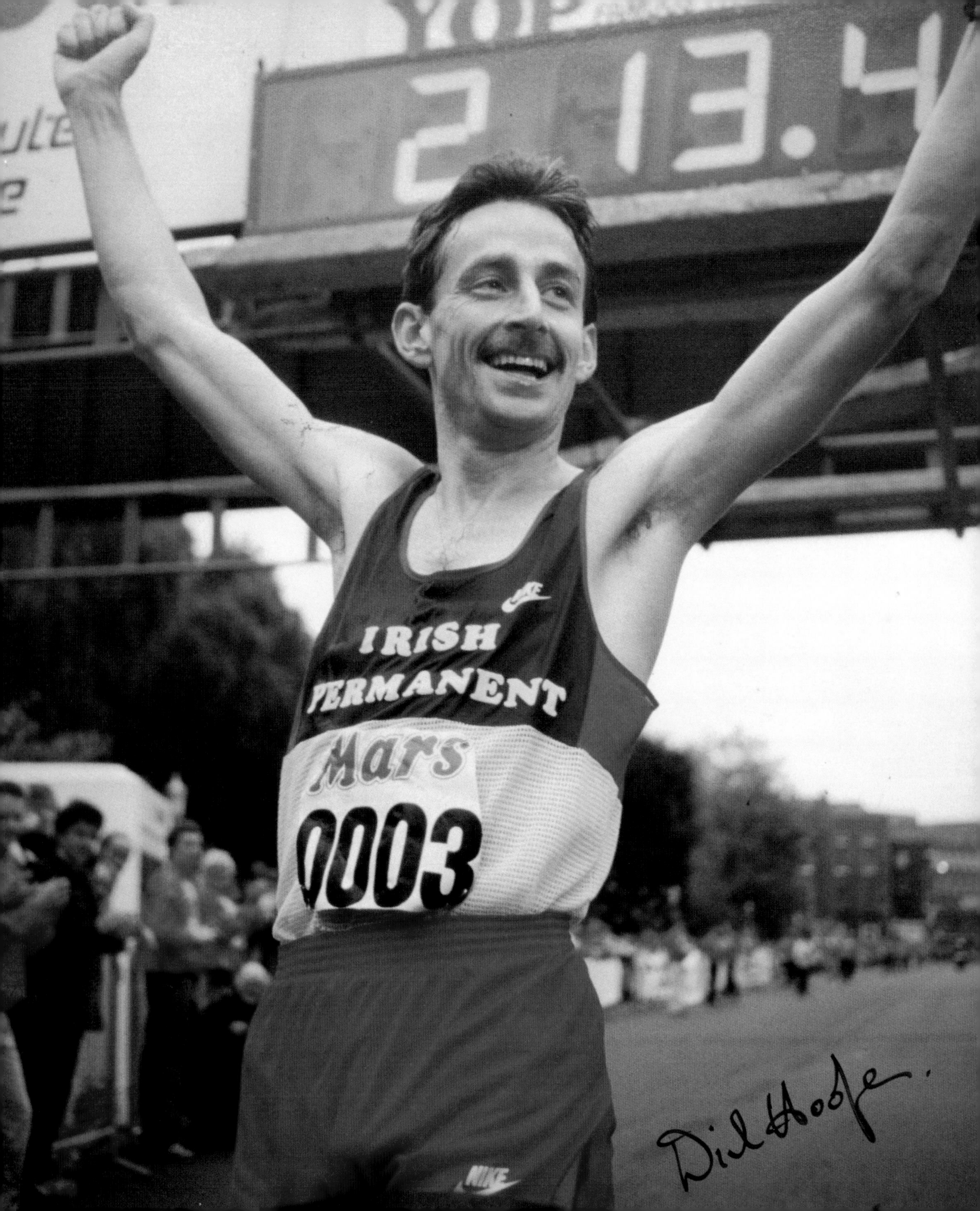
2 13.4
IRISH
PERMANENT
Mars
0003
NIKE

Foreword

In early 1980, I got a phonecall from the late Noel Carroll advising me of the proposed new Dublin City Marathon (as it was then known) modelled on the fast-growing and inclusive New York City Marathon. It was to be sponsored by the new fledgling radio station RTE Radio 2. He wanted to know if I would compete in the event. He was pushing an open door.

I had run in the Boston Marathon the year before. It was my first experience of a mass-participation marathon and I was overwhelmed with the atmosphere, the crowds, the support, the tradition. The event was won by a Bostonian, Bill Rodgers, who was to win it four times in all. Rodgers was a legend locally, known simply as 'Boston Billy'. It showed me the enormity of winning such a big event in your home city.

When Noel rang, all I could see was opportunity. Here was a chance for me to be Dublin's equivalent of Boston Billy. Luckily my vision came to pass and I won that first Dublin Marathon on the first ever Marathon Monday. The fact that for all three of my victories the race went through my native Raheny with me at the helm was the stuff of dreams. Before 1980, running the roads of Dublin was a risky business, runners were considered oddities and would often be subjected to verbal abuse. Now thousands of people were cheering me on and calling my name – it was nerve tingling and intoxicating.

Now, almost forty years on, the Dublin Marathon is this huge, prestigious event firmly established on the Irish sporting calendar and – more importantly – loved and appreciated by the people of our capital city. It is one of those annual events, like the St Patrick's Day parade, where the people involve themselves as participants, supporters and volunteers, simply because that is what you do on Dublin Marathon Day.

Dick Hooper winning the Dublin Marathon for the second time in 1985.

I'm honoured to pen a foreword to this valuable, well-researched and well-written history of the first forty years by my friend and clubmate Sean McGoldrick. Undoubtedly the event is now stronger than it has ever been. Demand to participate exceeds supply. The event has been embraced by the city and its people. It has not always been so. Long may all concerned appreciate what has happened.

I have been lucky enough to have a reasonably successful running career, competing in Olympic Games and winning national titles. Invariably, though, when in company I find myself being introduced as the chap who won the Dublin Marathon back in the day. I'm happy to live with that.

Dick Hooper, 2019

John Treacy winning the World
Cross Country Championship at
Green Park Racecourse, Limerick,
1979. Treacy went on to win a silver
medal in the Olympic Marathon
in LA in 1984. He won the Dublin
Marathon in 1993 in his final race
over the distance.

Chapter 1

Blame It All On Pheidippides

FATE, circumstances and serendipity all played their part in the birth of the Dublin Marathon in 1980. It was an idea whose time had come, though nobody involved in the inaugural Radio 2 Dublin City Marathon could have envisaged that forty years later the event would sell out in forty days.

A 26.2 mile run through the streets of Dublin wasn't the only innovation to come on stream in 1980. Ireland's first ATM opened; CIE's first bus lane came into operation on Parliament Street in Dublin city centre and *The Sunday Tribune* newspaper was launched. Melia Carroll was appointed the country's first female High Court judge, the future Pope Francis studied English here for three months and Johnny Logan's victory in the Eurovision Song Contest was celebrated in style. In sport, Kerry won their third All-Ireland title in a row while Galway won their first All-Ireland hurling title since 1923.

The running boom had yet to hit Ireland. Nevertheless, it was a heady time at the elite end of the sport. The athletic community was basking in John Treacy's memorable victory in the World Cross Country Championships on a never-to-be-forgotten afternoon at Green Park Racecourse, Limerick in March 1979.

Paradoxically, the idea for staging a city marathon in Dublin came from somebody who had no involvement in athletics. Louis Hogan, then a senior producer with RTE Radio, was on holiday in New York in October 1978. While out for a stroll, he noticed the runners in the city's annual marathon.

'I just saw the race by accident. I was walking down the street and there were a fair few people out watching it. The next day I read in the papers about an attempt being made to turn the event into a mass-participation marathon aimed at the common man who had never run twenty-six miles in his life.'

Little did Hogan realise that this chance encounter would change not just his life, but

the lives of thousands of Irish people over the next four decades. Even though he had gone to College Park in the 1950s to see the legendary John Joe Barry run, he wasn't an athletics buff. He was an international cricket umpire.

He promptly forgot about his brief encounter with the New York Marathon when he returned to Dublin. But then his career took an unexpected twist.

Back in the late seventies, the heretofore somewhat austere and ordered world of Irish broadcasting was undergoing a revolution. Dozens of pirate radio stations had sprung up, particularly in Dublin. Even though they were illegal, they were challenging Radio 1's dominance of the market and its listenership.

RTE's response was to establish a new pop music station, Radio 2, which was launched on 31 May 1979. Hogan, together with a number of other senior producers, was seconded from Radio 1 to get the new station – featuring its catchy slogan 'Radio 2, comin' atcha!' – established. Part of his remit was to formulate a strategy to promote the new station in Dublin, where the pirate stations had grabbed a big audience share.

'I remembered what I saw in the New York Marathon and I thought that maybe something similar could be organised in Dublin. But I hadn't a clue about athletics.' However, he knew somebody who did. His name was Noel Carroll.

A native of Annagasan, County Louth, Carroll's athletic career began when he was a cadet in the Irish Army in the early 1960s. He was spotted by the famous athletic coach 'Jumbo' Elliott, who trained Ron Delany when he won the 1500m title at the 1956 Olympic Games in Melbourne.

Legendary Villanova athletics coach, Jumbo Elliott, who recruited Noel Carroll.

Elliott offered Carroll a scholarship to attend Villanova University, where Delany had been a student. Carroll blossomed in America, running a sub-four-minute mile and was the anchor for the team that broke the 4 x 800 yard relay world record in 1964. He also set a European indoor record for the 880 yards and competed in the 800m in the Tokyo Olympics the same year.

Four years later at the Olympics in Mexico City he ran in the 400m and 800m and won gold medals at the European Indoor Games in Prague in 1967 and Madrid in 1968. He held Irish, European and World records, won fourteen Irish championships and three British AAA titles. Even after he retired from international athletics he stayed in the limelight becoming the full-time spokesman for Dublin Corporation in 1972.

'Noel was a friend of mine,' recalls Hogan. 'He was in and out of RTE all the time in his role as public relations officer for Dublin Corporation. So I decided to bounce the idea of a Dublin marathon off him.

'I explained that I wanted a race that would cater for people who didn't necessarily belong to athletic clubs and who wouldn't have to pre-qualify. My preference was for the race to be kept away from what might be described as the athletic "establishment". I promised Noel that if he could find somebody to organise the race, it would be promoted on RTE radio and in the *RTE Guide*.'

Unbeknownst to Hogan, Carroll had been trying for some time to sell the idea of running a marathon through the streets of Dublin to commemorate the late Frank Duffy, a legendary figure in the Civil Service athletic club, who had coached Carroll when he competed in the 1968 Olympics.

Carroll was a member of Civil Service AC and on 18 March 1978 he presented his proposal to the club's eight-man executive, which included Willie Dunne, the club secretary, who had represented Ireland in the marathon at the 1960 Olympics. But they turned it down for logistical reasons.

Eighteen months later Hogan and Carroll set their plan in motion by asking their respective bosses, Michael Carroll Head of Radio in RTE and Frank Feely, the Dublin City Manager, to exchange correspondences about the proposed marathon. 'I thought it was a great idea,' remembers Carroll, who later ran in the event. Feely, too, was enthusiastic about the idea. Ultimately they both played a pivotal role in the development of the race, though it was far from being a done deal at this time.

Marathon running was unashamedly elitist up until the mid-1970s, not just in Ireland, but throughout the world. The idea that an ordinary man or woman would attempt to run a marathon – never mind complete one – was regarded as heresy in the admittedly closeted world of organised athletics.

The marathon had its origins in Greek mythology. In 490 BC, Pheidippides, a messenger was dispatched from Athens to Sparta – a distance of 150 miles – to summon help for the Athenians who were fighting off the invading Persians in the Battle of Marathon. The

Spartans were reluctant to join in the battle and Pheidippides returned home the next day. On the way he encountered the god Pan, who told him the gods were on the side of the Athenians. He raced on to Athens to relay the good news. 'Rejoice, we conquer,' he reportedly said and then dropped dead. His epic run has been commemorated annually since 1983 by the staging of the Spartathlon, a 153-mile ultra-marathon, in which competitors have thirty-six hours to complete the course.

Nearly 1,500 years after Pheidippides' exploits, the founder of the modern Olympics Baron Pierre de Coubertin travelled from Paris to Athens to make final arrangements for the inaugural Olympics in 1896. He was accompanied by a friend, Michel Bréal, a French philologist, who apparently liked dreaming up things for other people to do.

He suggested to the Greeks that they organise a race to commemorate Pheidippides' epic run with a more manageable route from the site of the Battle of Marathon to Athens' Panathenaic Stadium – a distance of twenty-five miles. The Greeks loved the idea and Bréal promised to buy a gold cup for the winner, who was a local water-carrier, Spryros Louis. He led home the eighteen starters in a time of 2 hours, 58 minutes and 50 seconds.

American competitors at the 1896 Olympic Games brought home news of the event and five months later the first ever New York City Marathon was held. John J. McDermott, an Irish-American won it. A lithographer by trade, he also won the inaugural Boston Marathon in 1897.

The current marathon distance of 26 miles and 385 yards was standardised at the 1908 Olympics in London. It ran from the lawns of Windsor Castle to the new White City Stadium in West London a distance of twenty-six miles. The finish was in front of the royal box from where Queen Alexandra watched. She made a late request to move the start back to the East Lawn of Windsor Castle, so the royal children – including two future Kings of England – could watch from their nursery. This added an additional 385 yards to the course.

This race is one of the most infamous in Olympic history. Italian Dorando Pietri finished first, but was disqualified because he was helped over the finish line by spectators after he collapsed twenty yards short of it. The gold medal was awarded to Nenagh-born John Joseph Hayes. He was running for the United States having emigrated to New York with his family in 1894.

At the 1912 Olympics in Stockholm, Antrim-born Kennedy McArthur won the gold medal in the marathon, running in the colours of his adopted country South Africa. Seven decades later the event continued to be the sole preserve of elite male runners with interna-

tional success for Irish marathoners at a premium.

Limerick native Jim Hogan was in the lead group for most of the Tokyo Olympics in 1964 before dropping out four miles from the finish. Reporting on the event for the *Irish Times*, Ronnie Delany commented that Hogan 'dropped out exhausted at the twenty-two-mile stage after a brave but futile effort to match strides with the champion Abebe [Bikila].'

Jim Hogan subsequently fell out with the Irish athletic authorities. He competed for Great Britain, winning the gold medal in the marathon at the 1966 European Championships in Budapest.

Another Limerick native, Neil Cusack, caused a sensation in the United States by winning the Boston Marathon in 1974, arguably then the most famous distance race in the world. The elite nature of marathon running at the time was underlined by the paltry field of 1,951.

The late Con Houlihan in his *Evening Press* column prior to the Montreal Olympics in 1976 contemplated the eternal question: 'Why would anyone want to run a marathon?'

'The generally-accepted answer is that all marathon runners are mad. But this is not so: we have known a few and they were, in every other respect, eminently sensible men.

They spoke rationally about such elemental topics as the weather and the turf (both kinds) and the way the potato was losing its traditional flavour that if enforced would have those responsible regarded as higher in the hierarchy of heinousness.

'The amount of work that underpins the marathon can be expressed in hours and miles, but figures hardly capture its reality. The true loneliness of the long distance comes when, as it is so often the case, he is training on his own,' wrote Houlihan.

By the mid-seventies the marathon revolution was fermenting, principally in the United States where Frank Shorter won the Olympic Marathon title in 1972 in Munich – the city of his birth. He was the first American to win the title since Johnny Hayes' success in 1908 and his triumph sparked a fascination for marathons in the US – not just among athletes, but the general public as well. His victory contributed to the declassification of the marathon from being a rather obscure elitist race into a people's event.

'Everyone saw Frank's victory in the Olympics and that got the ball rolling,' suggested Bill Rodgers, winner of four Boston Marathons between 1975 and 1980 and four consecutive New York City Marathons between 1976 and 1979. 'That's when America discovered the marathon,' said Rodgers in an interview with Ron Rubin for his biography of Fred Lebow published in 2004.

Frank Greally, founder of *Irish Runner* magazine, witnessed the birth of the running boom in the US while on an athletic scholarship at East Tennessee State University in the 1970s. He credits two men – Jim Fixx and Dr George Sheehan – for persuading millions of Americans to take up running. A star athlete at college, Sheehan served as a doctor with the US Navy before becoming a cardiologist. He returned to running at the age of forty-five, initially in his backyard, then running along a river road during his lunch break wearing long-johns and a ski mask.

Five years later, he became the first fifty-year-old to run a sub-five minute mile. He wrote a column for a local newspaper and later became medical editor for *Runner's World* magazine.

'George Sheehan was the first running guru. He explained in every man's language what running was about. He was very much a philosopher, he talked not just about the physical, but also the spiritual side of running,' explained Greally.

Jim Fixx convinced millions of Americans to take up jogging; his *The Complete Book of Running* published in 1977 became a bestseller. Tragically, Fixx died in 1984 at the age of fifty-two after suffering a heart attack while out jogging. He had a genetic predisposition for heart disease.

RTE RADIO 2 1981 COURSE DUBLIN CITY MARATHON
RTE RADIO 2₂

FINGLAS
WHITEHALL
CABRA
ASHTOWN
PHOENIX PARK
FAIRVIEW
KILLESTER
RAHENY
CHAPELIZOD
MATT TALBOT BRIDGE
MERRION SQUARE
BALLYFERMOT
INCHICORE
CRUMLIN
DRIMNAGH
START/FINISH
AT ST. STEPHEN'S GREEN

Louis Hogan and the
1981 Dublin Marathon
course map.

But even in the US runners were still reluctant to commit to running a marathon. Everything changed in 1976 when it was decided that the New York Marathon would be run through the city's five boroughs to mark the bi-centennial of US independence.

Little did anybody involved realise how this one decision would change the lives of millions of people. The 290,300 runners who have completed the last thirty-nine Dublin Marathons would almost certainly never have got the opportunity to run through the streets of Dublin had the New York Marathon not been moved out of Central Park.

Ironically Fred Lebow, the director of the New York Marathon, who has been credited with popularising marathon running worldwide, was initially against the concept of a city-wide marathon.

Born into an orthodox Jewish family in the province of Transylvania, in Western Romania, near the Hungarian border, Lebow was originally known as Ephraim Fishl Lebowitz. The family were forced to split up and flee their home during the Second World War. As a teenager he spent time in Clonyn Castle in Delvin, County Westmeath, which was used as a school and refuge for displaced Jewish children. Later he emigrated to the US.

In 1970, along with two hundred others, he competed in the Cherry Tree Marathon in New York. Unimpressed by the event, he set about organising a marathon later that year. The first New York City Marathon basically circled Central Park four times attracting just 127 entrants. Only fifty-five finished and the non-finishers included the two women participants.

Lebow was a born publicist and the following year the field had doubled in size. It included New Jersey-born marathon pioneer Beth Bonner, who became the first woman in the world to break three hours clocking a then-stunning time of 2:55.22.

By the mid-seventies the event's media profile was on the rise. In 1975, the *New York Daily News* featured a picture of the winner Kim Merritt on its front page.

Olympian Ted Corbett, President of the New York Road Runners' Club and George Spitz, a marathon enthusiast and friend of Lebow's, independently came up with the idea of expanding the race as a one-time event to celebrate the nation's bicentennial in 1976.

Corbett suggested having teams from each of the five boroughs compete for a New York City marathon championship. But Spitz mistakenly thought he had proposed a race covering the five boroughs and brought the idea to Lebow, who rejected it out of hand. According to Ron Rubin's biography, he thought the idea was so ridiculous he refused to give the proposition a second thought.

Lebow changed his mind after a prominent Manhattan politician Percy Sutton secured a sponsorship deal worth $25,000 from a real estate agent.

The first city-wide New York Marathon passed through Staten Island, Queens, the Bronx, Brooklyn and Manhattan and took place on 25 October 1976. Bill Rodgers led home a record 2,090 runners – four times the size of the field for the 1975 event.

A record 9,875 turned up for the 1978 marathon that Louis Hogan witnessed. A year later Chris Brasher ran the New York Marathon. He was a noted personality in British athletics. In 1954 he was a pacer for Roger Bannister when he broke the four-minute barrier for the mile. Then two years later Brasher won the gold medal in the steeplechase at the 1956 Olympics.

Writing in the London *Observer* about his experience in New York, Brasher's enthusiasm for the event was self-evident. 'To believe this story you must believe that the human race can be one joyous family, working together, laughing together, achieving the impossible. I believe it because I saw it happening. Last Sunday in one of the most trouble-stricken cities in the world, 11,532 men, women and children from forty countries of the world, assisted by one million blacks, white and yellow people, Protestant and Catholics, Jews and Muslims, Buddhists and Confucians, laughed cheered and suffered during the greatest folk festival the world has seen.'

He returned to the UK determined to organise a similar event in London. By then plans for the first Dublin City Marathon were well in train.

Pat Hooper, wearing the logo of his employers, PMPA, finishing fourth in the Dublin Marathon in 1981 in a time of 2:20.01.

Chapter 2

No Country for Joggers

Ireland in the 1970s was a rather inhospitable place even for the country's established athletes. Olympian Pat Hooper had to seek permission from his boss in the PMPA insurance company to run to and from work every day – a round trip of thirteen miles.

'I decided after the 1972 Olympics that if I wanted to go up another notch in my career I would have to start running to and from work. The personnel manager knew about running as his secretary was Eamon Coghlan's sister, Ann. Still, he was concerned about whether I'd be too tired to do my job.

'Once I got the go-ahead, I then had to have the guts to actually go out and do it. I always wore tracksuit bottoms. I wouldn't dare show a bare leg. I had rocks and sticks thrown at me.'

Within the existing athletic structure, the fun or recreational runner was a virtual non-entity. 'It was a tough time for anyone who just wanted to run for enjoyment. They wouldn't have been shown much mercy,' acknowledges Pat's brother, three-time Olympian Dick Hooper.

And marathon running was even more elitist. Before the launch of the Dublin City Marathon in 1980, only a handful of marathons were staged annually in Ireland. The two rival athletic bodies, Bord Luthchleas na hEireann (BLE) and the National Athletic and Cultural Association of Ireland (NACAI) hosted a marathon championship race. For decades the Dublin County Athletic Board organised a marathon between Finglas and Ashbourne, while in August 1979 there was an Ulster championship marathon in Letterkenny, County Donegal.

With the exception of the last, the others were the sole preserve of elite male runners who were registered members of athletic clubs. There was no room for women. As the late Noel Carroll once wrote: 'women would risk burning at the stakes if they even suggested running a marathon.' Jean Folan finally broke the glass ceiling in 1979 when she became the first woman to compete in the BLE National Marathon Championship, though it wasn't until the following year that the organisation awarded championship medals to women in the event.

There was genuine concern about the welfare of marathon runners. In the 1960s, marathoners had to undergo a medical before the race. In his biography *From Boghall to Bethlehem and Beyond: The Bertie Messitt Story*, written by his son Ray, Messitt recalled the protocol before the Finglas-Ashbourne marathon.

'We had first to go to Santry and wait for the doctor. He called us in, one at a time, took our blood pressure, checked our heart-rates and asked how much training we had done, when we had our last meal and so on.'

The irony, of course, was the single biggest factor impacting on the wellbeing of marathon runners was the official ban on consuming drinks except at designated locations.

At this time, nobody under twenty-five ran a marathon. Pat Hooper, though, broke the mould when, in 1975 at the age of twenty-three, he won the Dublin County Board marathon on his debut in a record time

Bertie Messit (58) leading the marathon at the Rome Olympics, 1960. The legendary Abebe Bikila from Ethiopia (11) won the race running in his bare feet.

of 2:25. There were twelve runners in the race.

Slow marathoners were treated like pariahs. Alex Sweeney, who played a pivotal role in the establishment of the Business Houses Athletic Association (BHAA), made his marathon debut in the 1976 Dublin County Board event.

'Just before the start an official announced that he couldn't guarantee there would be any officials around for those who didn't finish in under three hours. And that's exactly what happened.'

Sweeney finished second in 2 hours and 36 minutes. On his arrival back to the Clonliffe Harriers' clubhouse in Santry, he noticed that one of his club mates who had run in the race had not yet returned. 'I drove back out to Finglas and there he was sitting on the side of the road. He had finished in 3.20, but there was no official around when he crossed the line.'

At least he fared better than his Clonliffe clubmate, the irrepressible Billy Morton, who arrived back at Croke Park leading the 1935 National Marathon Championship only to discover the gates were locked.

So engrossed was everybody in the All-Ireland one-mile cycle race that nobody heard him banging on the gates. Eventually the gates were opened, but by then John Timmons had arrived and he beat Morton in a desperate race to the line inside the stadium.

Morton did win the Irish marathon title the following year in an impressive 2:48.56 which ought to have earned him the right to run in the Olympic Marathon in Berlin, but Ireland didn't send a team because of the split in the sport!

In truth, the vast majority of runners had no interest in running marathons. But the lack of shorter races – both cross country and on the road – created a vacuum which started to be filled by *ad hoc* races organised by workers in different companies in the Dublin area.

This led to the formation of the Business Houses Athletic Association (BHAA) to act as an umbrella organisation for these new events. The drive to establish the organisation came primarily from two men, Bertie Messitt – who ran in the 1960 Olympic Marathon in Rome – and Tommy McDonald, who were on opposite sides of the split in Irish athletics.

A number of attempts were made to establish races for company employees in the 1960s. In his biography, Messitt recalled how his Donore Harriers' clubmate Dermot Lynskey, who worked for Guinness, conceived the idea of an inter-firms cross-country race in 1965.

Lynskey asked Messitt to put together a team from CIE; Alex Sweeney assembled a team from cigarette manufacturer Player-Wills, who sponsored the event, while Brian Price

The inimitable Billy Morton of Clonliffe Harriers. Morton was the driving force behind the building of the athletics stadium in Santry that now bears his name. He won the National Marathon Championship in 1936, but missed out on competing in the Olympic Games in Berlin.

entered a team from Aer Lingus. Coincidentally, Messitt, Sweeney and Price were key fig-ures in the organisation of the first Dublin City Marathon. The cross-country race took place and was a big success, but it was a once-off event.

Teams representing Aer Lingus continued to take part in World and European airline cross-country championships. On the back of these events Brian Price decided to organise a cross-country race for employees of local companies in 1978.

'I was newly married at the time and we had no television. My wife and I spent a few nights going through the Golden Pages and writing down the names and addresses of a

Left: The Hooper brothers, Dick (left) and Pat admire an Ireland singlet.

Above: Frank Slevin, the first race director of the Dublin Marathon, plots its course.

couple of hundred Dublin-based companies. I wrote to their personnel managers inviting them to enter a team. We had about two hundred and fifty runners on the day, which was considered a huge field,' he remembers.

Given his background it was inevitable that Bertie Messitt was the go-to man for would-be runners in the CIE garage in Donnybrook. In his biography he recalled being approached by two work mates, his nephew Ivan Messitt, a bus driver, and his conductor Jimmy Kavanagh. They were doing some training and were curious about their fitness and asked if he could organise a race for them.

Other CIE workers attached to Donnybrook were running at lunchtime recalls Frank Slevin, who was secretary of the sports and social club there at the time. Messitt and Slevin went back a long way. The latter changed his birth certificate and joined the British Army when he was only sixteen. Born in 1942, he turned the two digit into a zero. He was posted to Germany with the Royal Irish Fusiliers. On arrival he discovered that another Irishman Bertie Messitt was a celebrity in the regiment due to his prowess as an athlete.

Apart from Slevin, Ivan Messitt and Kavanagh, others involved in the still embryonic Donnybrook AC included Paddy Roche, who ran with Donore Harriers, Derry city native Pat McCourt, Mick Whelan and Phil Murray.

According to his biography Messitt invited Jimmy Gore, another ex-member of Donore, attached to the Clontarf garage to recruit a team. Subsequently a five-mile cross-country race for the runners from the two garages was organised.

After a couple of inter-garage races, Donnybrook AC in September 1977 organised their first major event, a four-mile cross-country race open to company teams. They used the CIE Sports and Social Club in Coldcut, Ballyfermot, as race headquarters. Six teams turned up.

On Messitt's prompting, all the runners were treated to tea and sandwiches afterward, a heretofore unheard of initiative in races south of the border. Bertie had experienced this kind of hospitality when he travelled north while running with Donore. He recognised the social value of this exercise and in time it became the norm. Its impact can be gauged from the fact that refreshments, including Irish barmbrack, are still available at all BHAA races.

The Coldcut event was notable for another reason. Before the race a dog invaded the start area and when the dog owner turned up he introduced himself as Ciaran Looney who worked in Heuston Station. He offered to stay around and help and went on to become a key figure in the BHAA and the Dublin Marathon.

In 1978 Donnybrook AC organised a ten-mile road race from Bray to Donnybrook bus garage; it turned out to be hugely significant in the evolution of women's distance running in Ireland. At the 1980 Olympics in Moscow the longest track race for women was 1,500m.

In the Donnybrook event, Mary Butler exploded the myth that women would be unable to run longer distances. She began her running career while a student in UCD. 'Women's distance running was still in its infancy. The cross-country races were a mile and a half long and the longest track event was 1,500m. Then the 3,000m was brought in on an experimental basis when I was in third year.'

After leaving college, she worked as a copy taker in the RTE newsroom. A number of her male colleagues were participating in the ten-mile race organised by Donnybrook AC. She was invited to join them and agreed despite the fact that the most she had ever run was seven miles.

Permission was needed from the race director Frank Slevin to allow her participate. 'The Gospel truth is that we had no expectation that women would take part.'

'The race was handicapped,' recalls Mary. 'The fastest man, Olympian Bertie Messitt, was going off from scratch. Frank, being the gentleman he was, said I could start five minutes ahead of the slowest man. I'd no idea of their standard and they had no idea of mine and so off I went. I crossed the finishing line first. I won because of the handicapping. I wasn't by any means the fastest over the distance as I did it in seventy-five minutes.'

In 1978 Mary Butler needed permission from the race director to run a distance of ten miles; by 1982 this group of runners from Beechmount Harriers on the Falls Road in Belfast were ready to tackle the Dublin Marathon.

Meanwhile, McDonald was spearheading a drive to launch an athletic club in his work place, the Irish Meat Packers plant in Leixlip. A talented athlete, he won a hat-trick of NACAI marathon titles between 1975 and 1977. With a personal best of 2:23.20 he could mix it with the best in the country. But because he was a member of Dunboyne AC which was affiliated to the NACAI he could not compete against the top BLE marathoners.

As the number of Business Houses races grew the need to put a structure in place to oversee them became obvious. On Sunday 25 February 1979, the Business Houses Athletic Association was founded at a meeting in the canteen of the Linson Squibb pharmaceutical company – now called SK Biotek Ireland – in Swords following a cross country race.

The attendance included Bertie Messitt, Brian Price, Frank Slevin, Ciaran Looney, Ned Sweeney, Dominic Branigan, Pat Hooper, Paul Brady and Niall Mathews. Significantly, both sides of the athletic divide in Ireland, BLE and NACAI, were represented.

The first annual general meeting of the new organisation was held on September 24, 1979 in the then CIE Hall in Marlborough Street in Dublin city centre. 'We stopped letting people in when there were four hundred people in the hall,' recalls Alex Sweeney who was persuaded by Bertie Messitt to become chairman.

Even though he was only thirty-eight, Sweeney was a very experienced athletics adminis-

Some of the founding members of the BHAA at a 30th anniversary reunion, along with Annette Croke, who was Operations Director of the 1983 Dublin Marathon: Back row: Annette Croke, Frank Slevin, Paddy Lennon, Dominic Branigan, Pat Hooper. Front row: Bertie Messitt, Alex Sweeney.

trator having served as both Captain and President of Clonliffe Harriers. The other officers elected at the AGM were vice-chairman: Ciaran Looney (CIE Heuston Station), secretary: Paddy Lennon (Irish Meat Packers), assistant secretary: Cathal Convery (Aer Lingus), treasurer: Frank Slevin (CIE Donnybrook), registrar: Ned Sweeney (Irish Shell) and public relations officer: Mary Butler (RTE).

'It was interesting looking around the hall to see who was there and their motives for being there. I ended up chairing a committee which was made up of BLE, NACAI members and fellas who were neither.'

The BHAA grew at a pace nobody anticipated – particularly in Dublin. In the twelve months after the inaugural AGM, companies affiliated to the organisation staged twenty-seven events on the road, track and cross country involving close on seven hundred runners from over eighty firms. Top class athletes like the Hooper brothers, Gerry Finnegan and Jerry Kiernan were regular participants. But what set BHAA races apart was the fact that down the field runners could win prizes.

This was a revolutionary concept in Irish athletics as Pat Hooper explains, 'Before the BHAA there were only a handful of road races and all of them only had two team prizes. Donore and Clonliffe would clean up at every race and the rest of us never saw a sausage.'

The BHAA devised a grading system for teams and runners based on previous results. This gave everybody an opportunity to win individual and team prizes. Furthermore, Frank Slevin devised an ingenious system for recording results based on using separate chutes at the finish line and different coloured race numbers for runners depending on their category.

His attention to detail knew no bounds. One of the biggest races organised by Donnybrook AC was a six-mile cross-country event in St Brendan's College near Bray. Teams representing transport companies in Belgium and France participated. Given the vagaries of the Irish weather he got the local scout troop to erect tents at the end of each chute where officials could shelter from the elements while documenting the race number and finishing time of each competitor.

But the biggest challenge facing the fledgling BHAA occurred shortly after their formal inception.

DUBLIN CITY MARATHON

Chapter 3

Comin' Atcha Through the Streets of Dublin

Top: Noel Carroll running the first Dublin Marathon in 1980.

Bottom: The viewing platform in Merrion Square for the 1986 Dublin Marathon. Lord Mayor of Dublin Bertie Ahern (centre, in mayoral chain) is flanked by (l-r) Cllr Joe Burke, chairman of the RTE Authority John Sorohan and Dublin City Manager Frank Feely. Bertie Ahern gave the nation a new bank holiday on the last Monday in October that would become Marathon Monday.

Alex Sweeney had scarcely time to get his feet under the table in his new role as chairman of the Business Houses Athletic Association when he got a call from RTE.

'I was invited to RTE to meet Noel Carroll and Louis Hogan. I was wondering what they wanted as I already had enough on my plate.' He thought the latest row in Irish athletics might be the subject of his summons to RTE. However, Carroll and Hogan had something entirely different in mind.

'They asked me whether I would be interested in inviting members of the BHAA committee to get involved in organising a Dublin City Marathon. Personally I was delighted with the idea.

'The one thing on my mind was that if we were going to do it we would do it right. From the outset I wanted it to be an inclusive event like all our races. Some BLE officials later suggested we were looking after "geriatrics". Maybe we were, but we wanted to revolutionise the sport and get rid of its elitist tag.'

The BHAA's strategy paid off handsomely. In the last four decades it has catered for competitors of all ages and standards who would never have dreamt of taking part in mainstream athletic events organised by Athletics Ireland.

On 30 November 1979 Sweeney, together with Carroll, made their pitch to the full BHAA committee at a meeting in the CIE Hall in Marlborough Street. 'It was a huge thing to be thrown at us,' remembers Frank Slevin. 'But Bertie [Messitt] and I had an Army background. We knew a little bit about organisation, logistics, rules and regulations.'

The BHAA committee accepted the challenge; Carroll was added to the committee, together with Sean Foley (Linsons), Ken Lee (RTE), Des McInerney (RTE), Bertie Messitt (CIE Donnybrook) and Brian Price (Aer Lingus).

The first item on their agenda was a date for the proposed marathon. Bertie Ahern when Minister for Labour in 1977 had gifted the nation a new bank holiday on the last Monday in October.

Hogan felt it was the perfect day for the marathon. 'Basically it was a dead day so I said let's make it Marathon Monday.' There were no dissenters. Given the organisational acumen that he had demonstrated with Donnybrook AC, Slevin was an obvious choice as race director. Price was the chief marshal and course director. The nuts and bolts of organising the race fell to Slevin and Price who approached the project with admirable gusto.

Sweeney, meanwhile, was left with the hot potato of dealing with BLE, which ultimately turned into a three-year battle. At one point the then Taoiseach Charles Haughey intervened on behalf of BLE.

Nobody had any idea how many would compete in the first marathon, though the early omens were less than encouraging. On the day of the official race launch, the Republic of Ireland soccer manager, Johnny Giles, unexpectedly announced that he was quitting. Any hope that the marathon would be a splash in the national papers the next day disappeared in an instant.

Thanks to the influence of Hogan, RTE kept their side of the deal. A six-month training schedule was published in the *RTE Guide* while Radio 2 DJ Jimmy Greeley volunteered to run in the race. But arguably it was Noel Carroll's Monday evening slots on Jim O'Neill's *Drivetime* show that had the most impact. He provided advice particularly for first-time marathoners and answered listeners' written queries.

Following the success of the New York Marathon the numbers participating in the National and Dublin County Board marathons had started to rise, though the figures were still in the low hundreds.

Brothers Extraordinary — singlemindedness their key..

Marathon Course

RTE RADIO 2
DUBLIN CITY MARATHON

1980
(organised by BHAA)

Monday, 27th October, 1980

Souvenir Programme 30p

ACKNOWLEDGEMENTS

Before long it became evident that the new marathon would have a record field. The entries were opened and arranged manually by Mary Butler and Frank Slevin in the sitting-room of his home in Shankill. 'We had no computer so we had to create a paper trail,' he recalls. Butler also put together a race programme, which was printed by RTE.

Slevin and Price spent a lot of time together in the months leading up to Marathon Monday. Slevin didn't have a car at the time, but he usually worked a split day, which allowed him to hop on a bus and head out to Price's workplace in Dublin Airport.

'We would have our committee meetings every fortnight and coming up to the marathon we'd meet more often. It was a challenge; everybody played their part. For the first marathon things were pretty basic. We were all learning.'

RTE originally announced that the marathon would start and finish on the main road in the Phoenix Park, though it would go through the city centre. However, the route eventually agreed upon saw the race starting and finishing outside the Department of Foreign Affairs on St Stephen's Green. It also passed through Raheny, home of high-profile marathoners, Pat and Dick Hooper.

The Dublin Marathon Committee in the early days, below, including Billy Kennedy, Dave Lawless, Zia Whyte, Tom Cullen, John O'Reilly, Marian O'Connell, Marion Kavanagh, Ned Sweeney and Alex Sweeney.

Below: The finishers' medal in the 2019 marathon, which is bronze in colour and features the Ha'penny Bridge, commemorates the 1980 finishers' plaque.

Measuring the course presented another challenge. 'I drove around it in my car about twenty times getting different measurements. So we had a rough idea from the speedometer, but I wasn't sure how accurate the measurements were,' recalls Price.

'I raised it at a committee meeting and Noel [Carroll] was very casual about it, but I insisted on the course being accurately measured. So I went to engineers in Dublin Corporation. They measured the course I had mapped out using their scaled maps. I still wasn't entirely happy and I suspect the first course was a wee bit short. Certainly in the first year a lot of people got fast times.'

The first ever Radio 2 Dublin City Marathon took the following route beginning outside

the Department of Foreign Affairs on St Stephen's Green. Mile 1: Thomas Street; mile 2: Parkgate Street; mile 3: Main Road, Phoenix Park; mile 4: Junction to Ratra Corner, Phoenix Park; mile 5: Navan Road, Halfway House; mile 6: Navan Road No 159; mile 7: Junction of Broombridge and Lagan Road; mile 8: Finglas Road opposite Dairy; mile 9: Ballygall Road, junction with Jamestown Road; mile 10: Glasnevin Avenue No 126; mile 11: Collins Avenue West opposite school; mile 12: Collins Avenue No 250; mile 13: Collins Avenue East No 76; Halfway mile 13.1: Collins Avenue East No 32; mile 14: Howth Road No 352; mile 15: Watermill Road/Convent; mile 16: James Larkin Road, near entrance to St Anne's Park; mile 17 Clontarf Road no 247; mile 18: Clontarf Road; mile 19: Fairview Park (near bandstand); mile 20: Amiens Street Station; mile 21: Merrion Square; mile 22: Northumberland Road; mile 23: Merrion Road No 146; mile 24: Stillorgan Road/footbridge; mile 25: Morehampton Road No 55; mile 26: Leeson Street, Sugar Company; Finish: St Stephen's Green, outside Department of Foreign Affairs.

There were a myriad of other logistical issues to be addressed ahead of the 1980 race. It was essential to secure the co-operation of An Garda Síochána. Even though the race fell on a Bank Holiday, due to a quirk in the rostering system at the time there was a full complement of Gardaí on duty. The Gardaí have played a pivotal role in ensuring the safe passage of runners and spectators throughout the history of the Dublin City Marathon.

In the 2019 marathon nearly 1,500 stewards – mostly drawn from athletic clubs in the greater Dublin area – will be on duty. This is in stark contrast to 1980 when, due to the frosty relationship between the BHAA and BLE, the organising committee had to secure volunteers from other sources. Price made contact and later met representatives of local resident associations along the marathon route and they organised the nine water and sponge stations. Dublin Fire Brigade assisted by opening up on-street fire hydrants to provide the water, which was then poured into disposable plastic cups and onto the sponges.

Money was scarce. Gillette sponsored the first London Marathon in 1981 to the tune of £50,000 – they doubled the figure for the 1982 race – but in its inaugural year Dublin had to rely primarily on the £1.50 entry fee from participants. Even though RTE 2 had the naming rights for the event, they were the promoters rather than the race sponsors and this later became a bone of contention.

'Our role was in the dissemination of information about the marathon through the *RTE Guide* and on the radio,' said Hogan.

When financial issues were raised at committee meetings, Noel Carroll used to say that the Corporation donated the streets of Dublin free. However, the county manager Frank Feely ensured there were limited road closures, pot holes were filled and buntings erected along the route. The Corporation along with Cospóir and the National Sports Council made financial contributions towards the running costs.

But mostly it was a case of necessity being the master of invention. A neighbour of Price's was a manager in the Dublin office of Hertz Rent a Car. 'I asked him whether it would be possible to get a few cars to use on race day.

'We subsequently had a meeting and Hertz came onboard providing us with a dozen cars on race weekend. The company liked the idea so much that my neighbour was sent to their offices in other countries to explain their relationship with the Dublin Marathon. The following year they became the official car supplier for the New York Marathon.'

Through Timemark Ltd, a Dublin-based watch and jewellery distribution company, contact was made with Seiko who rigged up two analogue clocks – one showing hours and the other showing minutes and seconds for the race. The organisers also shipped a digital clock from England, which was secured on temporary scaffolding at the finish line.

The relationship between Seiko and Price and Slevin blossomed and led to the two men setting up a timing company called Race Management, which provided timing services to

It was 1980, and my dad Gerry Nolan of Crusaders AC had been training hard for the first Dublin Marathon – but on marathon morning, 27 October, my mum, Brenda Nolan (also a Crusader) started having labour pains. My dad – in his running gear – dropped her to the Coombe Maternity Hospital where they examined her and told my dad to go run the race everything was ok. My dad set off with peace of mind, but around mile twelve my aunt popped out on the course and told him he'd just had a baby girl! Dad completed his marathon in a super time of around 3 hours! I was that baby girl; I also have a love for running (though I'm not as fast as my dad) and am also a member of Crusaders AC. This year I am running the Dublin Marathon on my thirty-ninth birthday. Sadly my dad has had to stop running since a recent knee replacement, but he's training me for my marathon. I'm so excited about running this year and having my dad there to cheer me on.

Joanne Carey

other road and later cycle races in Ireland and abroad. Other new businesses emanated from the marathon.

The organisers needed public-address systems and portable cabins for administration and storage. A new company, Mobile Communications, was set up by the late Tom Loftus and Johnny O'Meara to meet the demand. Forty years later they continue to supply equipment to the Dublin Marathon and the Women's Mini-Marathon.

Portaloos were used for the first time at a road race in Ireland. They were sourced in the United States by a Dublin-based company owned by Tom Costello, who still supply porta-

Feeling the pinch! A shoeless runner in the Dublin Marathon.

loos to the marathon. The organisers hit one unexpected snag on race day with their temporary loos. 'The site on which the Conrad Hotel was subsequently built was vacant at the time and the fifty portaloos we hired were located on the site. But we didn't erect proper signage to show where they were and they were barely used on the day,' recalls Price.

Computer Services Limited, a subsidiary of the Smurfit Group, assisted with the results while the National Dairy Council supplied milk to the finishers. All finishers received a distinctive engraved copper plaque – the brainchild of committee member Ned Sweeney – which featured a picture of Dublin's oldest pedestrian crossing, the Ha' penny Bridge. It was manufactured by Copperart, a company based in Newry, County Down. The finishers' medal in the 2019 marathon which is bronze in colour and features the Ha'penny Bridge commemorates the plaque that was presented in 1980.

Even though the New York Marathon had demonstrated that the majority of participants could complete the distance without undue distress there were concerns about runners' well-being. Carroll flippantly dismissed these worries by pointing out that runners would pass several hospitals on the route.

Two hundred volunteers from the St John Ambulance were on hand to provide first aid and medical assistance. A medical team headed by Dr Tom Cleary was on site while the Irish Heart Foundation provided four cardiac ambulances. There were no significant casualties during the event, though ten athletes and one spectator were taken to hospital.

Slower runners were provided with blinking armbands mindful that it could be dark by the time they finished. The last finisher crossed the line at 5.45pm as dusk was falling.

Communications on race day were crucial, but Slevin hit an unexpected hitch when he approached the Defence Forces seeking their expertise. Due to the troubles in Northern Ireland, most of the Irish Army's Signal Corp were on border duty. 'We found a radio association called the Amateur Radio Society of Ireland (ARSI) and with due credit to William Boles and George Adjaye they gave the race great cover from all parts of the route.'

In an *Irish Runner* article published in 1983, Price recalls how methodical the preparations were. 'Frank Slevin said we would need drink stations, medical personnel, a fleet of ambulances and buses, time-keepers all over the place, and a radio communications system to co-ordinate the whole thing. In addition, small armies of Civil Defence personnel, Boy Scouts and Girl Guides would be needed, as well as a team of competent officials to handle recording the results.

'Most of us did not think all this was really necessary, after all it was only a marathon we were organising. But Frank insisted that we were going to need it if the job was to be done properly.'

Six months before the inaugural Dublin Marathon, Slevin dispatched Price, Carroll and Paddy Lennon on a reconnaissance mission to observe the Peoples' Marathon in Solihull in Birmingham. 'Much to our

Official starter, Ciaran Looney, fires the starting gun.

The men who led the Smurfit Computing team that, in conjunction with Data General and Seiko Timing, tabulated the marathon results in 1982. Brendan Doyle (left) and Willie Morrison (right). As well as programming the data, Willie was the first Scotsman home in a time of 3:06.11.

amazement, a carbon copy of the "Slevin Scheme" was in full operation there and moreover, we realised that every detail was very necessary.'

The mainstream press were slow to embrace the marathon project in terms of affording it column inches. Three months ahead of the race, the *Irish Independent*'s athletics correspondent Tom O'Riordan, one of the country's elite distance runners who competed in the Tokyo Olympics, wrote a feature about the event.

He expressed reservations about the wisdom of staging a mass-participation marathon. 'Many people might argue that the organisers could have started off with a ten-mile run – as distinct from a race. But the target for those setting out on the 26 miles 385 yards will be to set themselves a pace that would see them through to the finish.'

Noel Carroll was typically philosophical. 'Running a marathon is like climbing a mountain; no one asks you how long it took you to reach the summit. Finishing a marathon is a great achievement.'

On the closing date for entries in September, 1,950 completed applications had been received. A further forty-three late entries were published in the souvenir programme which cost 30p.

Seventy of the entrants were female – an unprecedented number considering that in the 1980 National Marathon the previous May only three women started and two, Jean Folan and Kathy Naughton, finished.

Registration for the first Dublin Marathon took place in Kevin Street College of Technology, which also served as the baggage drop centre. Dublin was the third capital city in the world, after Berlin (1974) and Stockholm (1979) to host a people's marathon.

An exhausted committee thought they had every angle covered. Carroll was confident enough to tell Tom O'Riordan in an *Irish Independent* interview on the Friday before the race 'there is a plan for every contingency.'

But they hadn't counted on the vagaries of the Irish weather. In the twenty-four hours prior to the race torrential rain fell throughout Dublin. So with considerable trepidation, Price sat into his car early on race morning to do one final reconnaissance of the course.

All was fine until he reached the nine-mile mark in Finglas. The Tolka River had overflowed its banks and part of the intended route was flooded. He rerouted the course and the runners did an unscheduled lap around St Stephen's Green at the start to make up the difference.

The approach on the day was quite relaxed. Race numbers were still being distributed in Kevin Street up to an hour before the scheduled noon start.

The enthusiasm at the start was infectious. So much so that when the countdown reached five, runners surged through the start line before Lord Mayor of Dublin, Alderman Fergus O'Brien TD, officially started the first ever Radio 2 Dublin City Marathon.

RTE AC in their club strip, 1981. Back Row l-r: Richie Lynch, Frank Hand, John Tynan, Peter Kennedy, Paddy Goode, Paddy Ryan, Michael Walsh, John O'Connell, Dermot McGrath. 3rd Row l-r: Kevin Linehan, Niall Mathews, Charlie Murphy, Bernard McManus, Mick Murray, John Kelleher, Jack Mitchell. 2nd Row l-r: Mick Bourke, Joe Graham, Gerry Kelly, Martin Moore, Dave White, Des McInerney, Mary Kennedy, Brian Dowling, Patrick Hogan. Front Row l-r: Billy Forde, Jim Carraher, Peter Dunne, Pat Kavanagh, Mary Butler, Malachi Lawless and son Isaac, Victor Curtis, Ian McGarry, Peader Dempsey.

Chapter 4

Hero for a Day

Top left: Marathoner Pat Hooper, who ran 5,990 miles in training in 1979 when he won the BLE National Marathon title.

Bottom left: The legendary Jim McNamara (213) of Donore Harriers leads a group, including Tom O'Riordan (210), who went on to become a sports journalist with the *Irish Independent*. Both McNamara and O'Riordan are Olympians.

DICK Hooper harboured ambitions of being an Olympic marathoner while still at secondary school in St Paul's College, Raheny. Four years younger than his brother Pat, he followed his lead and joined Raheny Shamrock AC when he was fifteen.

Success followed quickly. At the 1973 National Community Games finals, he won the bronze medal in the boys U-17 six-mile race. In 1974, he picked up two silver medals in the All-Ireland schools' championships in the cross-country and steeplechase events.

The following spring he was a member of the Irish team that finished second behind the US at the World Junior Cross-Country Championships in Rabat, though he missed out on the team medal as he was a non-scoring member.

Even then, his mind was on marathons as he explained in an interview with the late Jim Dowling published in the *Irish Runner* before the 1981 Dublin City Marathon. 'I started running marathons because I had Olympic ambitions and I did not feel I would ever reach the standard over 10,000m. I knew I had enough talent to make it at the marathon.

'I was very single-minded and independent. Once I started doing twenty-mile runs with Pat [Hooper] and Jim McNamara over the hill of Howth, I realised that the longer I ran the stronger I got. So I knew I had a talent for it and got quite organised in terms of my ambitions,' he now recalls.

Self-coached, he was strongly influenced by the writings of famed New Zealand coach Arthur Lydiard, who trained Olympic champions, Peter Snell and Murray Halbert along with Brian Magee, who won a bronze medal in the marathon at the Rome Olympics.

'From the time I left school my mind was made up that I would move up to the marathon. I wasn't afraid of the age thing,' said Hooper. In those days the majority of athletes didn't focus on the marathon until they were in their late twenties.

He ran the Liffey Valley Half Marathon when he was seventeen, clocking a respectable

66.32. 'Two years later I ran it again in 65.20. So I had kinda arrived at that stage as I could break fifty minutes for ten miles. In 1977, I won the Clonliffe Harriers twenty-mile road race in 1:42.48, which was significant as well. But I resisted the temptation to run a marathon later that year.'

Instead, he bided his time making a winning marathon debut at the 1978 BLE National championships in Tullamore in 2:23.19. His victory caused a sensation in the tightly knit Irish marathon community. At twenty-one, he was the youngest ever winner of the title, though his time was the slowest since Jim McNamara crossed the line to take the title in 2:24.29 in 1966. In 1976 Danny McDaid won the title in 2:13.06.

But the 1978 race was run in sweltering heat and only nineteen of the 102 starters finished. Hooper's punishing training regime, which included two thirty and thirty-two-mile runs, allied to his precision planning set him apart from his rivals. He had driven the course and had a team of helpers who ensured his drinks were available out on the course.

His older brother Pat finished second and the pair ran in the European championships the following September. Pat finished twenty-seventh in 2:20.28. Dick was twenty-ninth in 2:21.00.

Carey May didn't have any burning ambition to run a marathon during her teenage years. Born in Portsmouth in 1959, her family came to Ireland when she was eleven and settled in Ticknock in the foothills of the Dublin Mountains.

She competed in the long jump and hurdles at schools' level with Wesley College. Orienteering was her first sporting passion and she competed for Ireland at

Left: Carey May in the 1980 Dublin Marathon.

Dick Hooper (no number), the eventual winner, with his brother Pat (220), runner-up, leading the pack which includes Danny McDaid (white cap, left), Norman Deakin (peaked cap), Jim McNamara, Philip English, Paddy Coyle, Mick Byrne, Sean O'Flynn, Gerry Hannon, Mick Woods, Neil Cusack, Tony Kearns and Tony Conroy in the early stages of the 1980 BLE National Marathon Championship.

the 1979 World orienteering championships in Finland.

In her first foray into distance running she finished ninth in the 1978 Dublin Cross-Country Championships. After a couple of top ten finishes in the National Cross Country, she earned her first international vest in the now defunct Home Countries Cross Country in 1979.

Her first experience of a marathon came in 1980 when she followed the BLE National championship event in Tullamore on a bicycle.

Even though more than a decade had passed since Kathrine Switzer famously defied the authorities to finish the Boston Marathon, this was the first time BLE had incorporated a women's event in the National Marathon. Winner Jean Folan, Mary Walsh and Kathy Naughton were the only female participants.

May's interest had been piqued, though she now acknowledges her foray into marathon running was a combination of a spontaneous notion, hot-headed ignorance of the challenge and the 'don't tell me I can't do something' attitude.

'I wanted to run in Tullamore, but I had a hip injury after the cross-country season. Seeing a marathon for the first time does inspire you. It is so different from any other event,' May told Jim Dowling in a subsequent *Irish Runner* interview.

'Training for my first few marathons was very unscientific. Although I competed in athletics all through school, I hadn't run much further than 400 metres over hurdles. It was through orienteering and training with two good friends, Declan O'Callaghan and Eoin Rothery, that we came up with the hare-brained idea to run a marathon,' she recalls.

In August 1980, Letterkenny hosted the Ulster Open Marathon. There were forty-five finishers, but it was May's sensational debut performance which caught everybody by surprise.

She finished nineteenth in 2 hours, 53 minutes and 18 seconds, more than twenty minutes faster than the 3:16 set by Bridget Cushen, an English-based Irish runner who is credited with being the first Irish female to complete the distance.

'It was a spur of the moment decision,' May recalls. 'I don't think I told my parents. They were used to me taking off to orienteering events and run races. I was pretty independent and

although they didn't always know what I was up to, I do know they were proud of my accomplishments.

'Declan, Eoin and I were training for orienteering events and saw the advert for Letterkenny. We were in awe of Danny McDaid and thought it would be cool to go to his home town and try a marathon. I'm not sure that I was even aware of the Dublin Marathon at that stage or that I would ever run another one. We all worked full-time, rode bikes to training and didn't take it more seriously than it seemed to warrant at the time.

'The only specific training run I did was an approximate twenty-mile run beside the car the lads drove to Wexford. We estimated it was at about six-minute pace. So I figured another six miles was totally doable. It was very unscientific and haphazard. But the idea of breaking three hours for 26.2 miles was firmly cemented in my brain.

'We drove up to Letterkenny from Dublin the night before the race. The kitchen was closed in the bed and breakfast, so we had beans on toast. Later we went to the local fair ground, got really dizzy on the rides, then up the next morning and ran a marathon.'

My love affair with the Dublin City Marathon started with the very first one, back in October 1980. I was ten years old and my family had driven from Skerries to Raheny. I can clearly remember the bulletins on the radio about the progress of the race. We pulled into a lane near Watermill Road and my dad and I ventured down to see the runners passing by. I clearly remember Dick Hooper (the winner of the first Dublin Marathon) coasting past in his green and white shorts on winning the first Dublin Marathon. I decided that day that I was going to be a runner. In 1997 I took up the challenge and ran my first Dublin Marathon. The emotions were incredible – I was now one of those heroes! I met Dick Hooper when we were spectating at the Rio Olympic Games in 2016, and told him that watching that first race in 1980 moulded me into the person I am today.

Alan Worral

Bottom left: Donegal man and two-time Olympian Danny McDaid of Clonliffe Harriers running the Dublin Marathon in the 1980s.

Dick Hooper first heard about a marathon being run through his native city in a phone conversation with Noel Carroll about six months before the race. He was smitten straight away.

'I jumped at the idea because I knew it was going to be big. I had run in the Boston Marathon in 1979. The whole event revolved around Bill Rodgers who won it for the third time that year. Everything was Bill, Bill, and Bill. I fancied being the Bill Rodgers of Dublin.'

Hooper was unbeaten on Irish soil in marathons. He won the national title for a second time in May 1980, again in Tullamore, with his brother Pat – who had won the title in 1979 – finishing second. Pat's chances of winning weren't helped when a well-meaning spectator threw a bucket of water over him in the searing heat at the twenty-mile mark.

Three months later in Moscow they became the first siblings to compete in the same Olympic marathon. Neither was satisfied with their performance. Dick was thirty-eighth in 2:23.53; Pat finished forty-second in 2:30.28.

The latter got married a week before the Dublin Marathon so Dick was carrying the family colours in the race, having turned down an opportunity to run in the New York Marathon. 'The Olympic marathon was on August 1 so I had twelve weeks to get myself right. And I had committed to the race.'

In the wake of her breakthrough win in Letterkenny, twenty-one-year old May – then a member of Dublin City Harriers – was aware of the expectations that surrounded her. 'The pre-race jitters were quite strong. I got a lift into Stephen's Green and was excited to try out a new pair of runners. Again I didn't have too much experience on how to prepare

for marathons,' she says, an acknowledgement that she broke one of the cardinal rules of running: never wear brand new runners in a marathon.

There are exceptions to every rule and she was clearly made from a different mould. Furthermore, she was blissfully unaware of who her rivals would be. 'I honestly didn't know any of the other female competitors. The first marathon I was aware who my competitors were likely to be was in Cork (at the BLE National Marathon Championships in 1981) when Emily Dowling was running.'

The female entrants included Mary Butler, who was public relations officer for the race. The previous August she clocked 3.26 in the all-women's Avon Marathon in London. Avon Cosmetics were campaigning at the time to have a marathon for female athletes included on the Olympics programme. The campaign was the brainchild of Kathrine Switzer of Boston Marathon fame.

The London race had symbolic significance as it was held two days before the men's marathon at the Moscow Olympics. The campaign had a successful conclusion with the women's marathon added to the programme for the 1984 Olympics in Los Angeles. This would impact significantly on the future direction of May's life. But on that Monday morning in October 1980 she was focused on running 26.2 miles through the streets of Dublin.

There was no real form guide in the women's race. But Hooper was the obvious front runner in the men's race, though curiously the pre-race coverage scarcely mentioned the likely battle at the front of the field. Instead, under a banner headline 'It's a mad, mad

Left: Neil Cusack, from Limerick, in full flight. Cusack won the Boston Marathon in 1974, the only Irish athlete ever to do so.

Right: runners in the inaugural Dublin Marathon, including Eamon Ryan (595), John Laurence Rigney (583) and Desmond Cunnane (859).

Conor Faughnan
Director of Consumer Affairs for AA Ireland

Long before he was the public face of the Automobile Association in Ireland Conor Faughan had another claim to fame. He was one of the youngest finishers in the 1981 Dublin City Marathon completing the course at the tender age of twelve.

He wasn't particularly interested in athletics, but he took on the race as a personal challenge. 'I remember the RTE Guide published a training programme that began with a ten-minute run and worked its way up to a marathon after four or five months.

'I did the first day, did the second day and made a habit of it. It took my parents weeks to realise I was serious. I think they said little because they were sure it would wear off quickly. It didn't because I was a stubborn little sod. The more people told me I couldn't do a marathon the more determined I became.'

Another challenge faced him as he was attending boarding school in the Cistercian College, Roscrea where rugby was the only sport that counted. 'I could skip rugby, armed with a note from my parents about my (marathon) training which set me apart as a bit of an oddball.'

The enormity of the crowds on the course in the 1981 race has stayed with him ever since. 'All the weeks of lonely running and now the streets were lined ten deep and every single person supporting you. There was a group of nurses who were running and they sort of adopted me for a stretch, much to my delight.

'I also remember hitting the wall. Miles 20 to 22 were horrific, but by mile 26 I felt so fresh I thought I could do another lap,' said Faughnan, who was taken aback by the reaction afterwards in school.

'I went from an eccentric oddball to a genuine sporting achiever. When I did the marathon again the following year two other students joined me.'

Although he retired from marathon running at the age of thirteen he believes the experience had a lasting impact on his life.

'It taught me about setting goals and achieving them, about being able to completely ignore doubters and those who would hold you back. It also taught me that you can approach any large task and break it down into pieces, stick to it with determination and you will get it done.

'I think it was very positive and formative for things like wellness and esteem issues that are better understood now than they were then.

'I got a lifelong physical legacy out of it too. I have always held a base level of fitness and stamina despite many years of bad habits afterwards. There has never been a time when I wasn't reasonably trim and aerobically fit, even now.'

Nowadays entrants have to be eighteen on race day in order to compete.

marathon Monday,' the *Irish Independent* focused on the logistical challenges of staging the biggest ever mass-participation sporting event in Ireland.

The mood was captured by Tom O'Riordan who wrote: 'This race is not so much about stars or fast times as participation and a sense of achievement. And it will be a great sense of achievement for the vast majority.' Twenty-one years later, O'Riordan's son, Ian, who carried on the family athletic and journalistic traditions with the *Irish Times*, finished twenty-third in the race in 2:31.09.

Hooper regarded Neil Cusack as his biggest threat. The Limerick Olympian caused a stir among the elite runners when he turned up sporting a logo for Kentucky Fried Chicken on his singlet. He had negotiated a sponsorship deal worth £3,000 with Limerick businessman Pat Grace, who owned the franchise for KFC in Ireland.

This was a first in Irish athletics. It was another headache for BLE and generated much debate among the other elite runners. 'The word went around fairly quickly that he was

cleaning up on the deal. We didn't know what he was getting, but everybody was adding noughts to the figure,' recalls Hooper. By the time the next Dublin Marathon came around all the leading runners were sporting logos on their singlets.

Hooper respected his Limerick rival, but believed he had his measure over the longer distances. 'Around that time I could never beat him in a short race, but he never beat me in a long one so that gave me great confidence whenever I lined up against him in a marathon.'

As was his wont Hooper's preparations were meticulous. Not alone had he driven the course, he had run most of it. 'The route was firmly implanted on my mind.'

By the fifteen-mile mark, the lead pack had been reduced to two, Hooper and Donore Harriers' Jim McGlynn. Hooper made his move a mile later as they raced along the coast road near Clontarf, where he had logged thousands of training miles. From there he ran solo, crossing the finishing line on St Stephen's Green in 2:16.14, thirteen seconds inside his personal best.

'This was very important for me. I was shattered after Moscow and needed that win to show that I am back on course,' he told reporters afterwards. It was a memorable day for the family. His brother Pat was co-commentator for the race with John Saunders which was broadcast live on Radio 2.

McGlynn dropped out and Cusack took the runner-up spot in 2:20.40 while Cork's John O'Flynn took the other spot on the podium. For the race winner it was a day unlike any other before or since. 'Going in the race was the best decision I ever made. If I never do anything else in my life I will always be remembered as the fella who won the first Dublin Marathon.'

Meanwhile, out on the course, May was having quite the day. 'I went out with a group of men and got into a rhythm.'

She possessed an innate confidence, which in a later life she tried to instil in the high school kids she coached in the US. 'I would describe it as a "quiet confidence" where you never go talking about how you're going to win, but you quietly know you are and no one is going to beat you. Obviously that isn't always the case, but it's a way to tell yourself to be the best you can be and no one is going to mess with that.'

There was no sign of any other females so May just concentrated on her own race. 'I remember turning onto the dual carriageway beside RTE and Roy Dooney (a DCH club-mate) yelled at me that I was on pace for 2:42.

'There weren't great timing facilities along the route so that was good news, I knew there were six miles to go and I just had to keep pushing.' But she encountered an unexpected problem a couple of miles from the finish. A male spectator tried to impede her progress.

'An old guy came out of the crowd and pushed and shouted at me that a girl shouldn't be running a marathon. It was disconcerting because I was very tired and it threw me off my stride.

'I knew the finish was very close though, so I kept on pushing. I wasn't going to let an old guy stop me. The finish was phenomenal. It was such a relief and I felt like I was sprinting down the Green. I'm sure I wasn't, but it felt like it.'

She smashed her own Irish marathon record with a time of 2:42.11. The win transformed not just her athletic career, but her life. The following year she left her job as a computer data processor in UCD, to take up an athletic scholarship in Brigham University in Utah.

For forty years she never told anybody about her encounter with the male spectator. 'I was so excited about winning I probably forgot about the incident and anyway I didn't

Right: The printed results of the first Dublin Marathon, 1980.

PLACE	NAME/TIME
1	Hooper Dick (02 16 14)
2	Cusack Neil P (02 20 40)
3	O'Flynn John S (02 26 33)
4	Hodgins Dick (02 28 01)
5	O'Shea Brendan (02 28 09)
6	McGrath Ciaran (02 28 10)
7	O'Connor John (02 29 13)
8	Ryan Tony (02 29 29)
9	Cardiff James (02 31 15)
10	Woods Stan (02 31 17)
11	Whelan John P (02 32 37)
12	Talbot Ian K (02 32 44)
13	Murphy Patrick B (02 33 16)
14	Connolly Philip (02 33 34)
15	McGrath Mattie (02 34 26)
16	Treacy Christy (02 34 38)
17	Doyle Laurence John (02 35 14)
18	Scanlan Joseph (02 35 25)
19	McKeon Michael (02 35 50)
20	Seaton David C (02 35 51)
21	O'Dowd Paraic (02 35 52)
22	Power Con M (02 36 36)
23	Jordan Thomas G (02 36 51)
24	McNamara James (02 37 02)
25	Dunne William (02 37 07)
26	Cregan Seamus (02 37 11)
27	O'Connell Pat (02 37 17)
28	Heffernan Patrick G (02 37 34)
29	McGrath Edward (02 38 24)
30	McGonigle Desmond J (02 38 30)
31	McCarthy Dermot A (02 38 31)
32	Browne Frank (02 38 35)
33	Young Walter (02 38 36)
34	Carroll John (02 38 47)
35	O'Leary John J (02 38 51)
36	Brennan Andrew G (02 38 59)
37	Holland Tom (02 39 02)
38	Kinsella Raymond P (02 39 44)
39	Culligan Michael John (02 39 47)
40	Kerr Harry (02 39 53)
41	King James J (02 40 23)
42	Delaney Paul (02 40 29)
43	Burke Donal A (02 40 31)
44	McCarthy Joseph J (02 40 42)
45	Treacy Michael M (02 40 57)
46	O'Reilly John (02 41 12)
47	Brady Donald (02 41 31)
48	Durnin Patsy (02 41 33)
49	O'Leary Flor (02 41 36)
50	May Carey (02 42 11)
51	McElroy Colm (02 42 47)
52	Byrne Seamus J (02 42 54)
53	Spillane Edward (02 43 06)
54	Walshe John (02 43 30)
55	Roche Michael (02 44 12)
56	Kiely Denis J (02 44 21)
57	Goulding Ham (02 44 27)
58	Redican Thomas (02 44 28)
59	O'Dwyer Kieran (02 44 36)
60	Sweeney Alex J (02 44 43)
61	Graham George (02 45 09)
62	Curtin Timothy G (02 45 28)
63	Ward Patrick (02 45 48)
64	O'Donoghue Patrick (02 46 01)
65	McKay William J (02 46 02)
66	Murphy Noel Patrick (02 46 05)
67	Costigan Liam (02 46 06)
68	Moran Gerard (02 46 15)
69	Kinahan Thomas O (02 46 43)
70	Sharkey Thomas (02 46 47)
71	Brannigan William A (02 46 52)
72	Walsh Patrick (02 46 59)
73	Purcell Frank (02 47 01)
74	O'Driscoll Tom (02 47 16)
75	Daunt Clive A (02 47 17)
76	Pender John J (02 47 56)
77	Twomey Tadgh (02 48 08)
78	Madden Tom (02 48 10)
79	Byrne Desmond A (02 48 19)
80	Hoey Michael J (02 48 27)
81	McCourt Patrick (02 48 37)
82	McGrattan Eamonn (02 48 43)
83	Reynolds Davy (02 48 54)
84	O'Connor Michael (02 48 55)
85	McGrath Patrick Anthony (02 48 56)
86	Foley Thomas (02 49 09)
87	King Anthony (02 49 42)
88	Gatenby Robin (02 50 07)
89	Kavanagh Jerry (02 50 20)
90	Whelan Robert (02 50 21)
91	Duignam Robert J (02 50 23)
92	Alcorn Robert (02 50 56)
93	Campion Loughlin J (02 51 30)
94	Downey Bernard (02 51 53)
95	Hayes Jerry (02 51 54)
96	Kelly Aidan (02 51 57)
97	Haxby James B (02 52 17)
98	Craddock Patrick (02 52 22)
99	Murphy Donal Francis (02 52 34)
100	Lyons Jeremiah Patrick (02 52 46)
101	Fleming Thomas (02 52 47)
102	Coady Kevin A (02 52 54)
103	Bourke Michael F (02 53 06)
104	Carmody Brian (02 53 18)
105	Marley Paddy (02 53 19)
106	Devine Willie (02 53 32)
107	Cunningham Robert (02 53 35)
108	McMahon Eamonn (02 53 40)
109	Mulvey James P (02 53 47)
110	McCabe James (02 53 55)
111	Roche Patrick (02 54 04)
112	Crimin Michael (02 54 19)
113	Tsigdinor Karl A (02 54 35)
114	Ennis Tony (02 54 43)
115	Messitt Albert John (02 54 45)
116	Wright Stephen (02 54 51)
117	Gash Hugh (02 55 02)
118	Hogan James Bernard (02 55 04)
119	Langan John (02 55 07)
120	Duffy Seamus (02 55 12)
121	Geraghty Donal (02 55 14)
122	Dwyer William (02 55 28)
123	Stewart James Francis (02 55 35)
124	O'Halloran Hugh (02 55 38)
125	Clifford D C (02 56 07)
126	Malone George (02 56 14)
127	Macey Timothy (02 56 15)
128	Power James M (02 56 19)
129	Carmody Paul (02 56 20)
130	Grace Patrick A (02 56 26)
131	Brazil Denis (02 56 30)
132	Grant Colin (02 56 36)
133	O'Hanlon Martin (02 56 44)
134	Daly Noel Patrick (02 56 45)
135	Raftery Olaf (02 56 47)
136	Gill Frank (02 56 49)
137	Millington Kenneth A (02 57 12)
138	O'Shea Paschal (02 57 26)
139	Keane Barry A (02 57 28)
140	Urguhart Alan (02 57 33)
141	Mullany Sean (02 57 35)
142	Murray John M (02 57 43)
143	Gallagher Damien (02 58 02)
144	O'Donoghue Thomas (02 58 06)
145	Hoey Jack (02 58 10)
146	McDowell William (02 58 15)
147	Murray Patrick (02 58 16)
148	Byrne Gerry (02 58 34)
149	Swift Thomas (02 58 48)
150	O'Neill Patrick (02 58 50)
151	Clarke Noel (02 58 55)
152	Markey Peter (02 59 17)
153	Maguire Terry Dr (02 59 30)
154	Cawley Seamus (02 59 34)
155	Alton Seamus (02 59 39)
156	O'Reilly Patrick N (02 59 41)
157	Hendrick Kevin B (02 59 42)
158	Kellett Dominic (02 59 43)
159	Moore Joe (03 00 00)
160	Hughes Pat (03 00 27)
161	Jones Frank P (03 00 27)
162	Cullen Robert (03 00 35)
163	Madden Gerard M (03 00 37)
164	Cottney Derek (03 00 42)
165	Rigney Seamus (03 00 47)
166	Doyle Sean D (03 00 48)
167	Curry J P (03 00 49)
168	O'Riordan William (03 00 55)
169	McCullough John (03 01 16)
170	Barry Noel (03 01 22)
171	Kelly Owen (03 01 31)
172	O'Rourke Tommy (03 01 32)
173	O'Carroll Daniel (03 01 33)
174	McQuaid Finian P (03 01 45)
175	Corcoran Gerald (03 01 46)
176	McDaid Frankie Y (03 01 49)
177	Rooney Dominic (03 01 52)
178	O'Brien Sean (03 01 53)
179	McGinley Robert (03 02 07)
180	Brady Patrick (03 02 10)
181	Pierce William (03 02 18)
182	Kane Michael (03 02 26)
183	Walsh Mary (03 02 27)
184	Shannon Eamonn (03 02 32)
185	Bryson Robin (03 02 38)
186	Fahy Tony (03 02 45)
187	Lee Peter (03 02 53)
188	Fox Billy (03 03 06)
189	Hon Brenda (03 03 16)
190	Brennan Thomas (03 03 42)
191	Clooney Colm (03 03 45)
192	Collins David (03 03 46)
193	Murphy Marie (03 03 48)
194	Price John (03 03 59)
195	O'Brien Richard (03 04 05)
196	Phelan Noel (03 04 11)
197	Humphreys Kevin (03 04 22)
198	O'Callaghan Michael (03 04 32)
199	Ryan Gerard (03 04 35)
200	Williams Liam (03 04 42)
201	Fox John (03 04 47)
202	Christie Tony (03 04 49)
203	O'Sullivan Eugene (03 04 52)
204	McInerney Noel (03 04 53)
205	Byrne Eamonn (03 05 00)
206	Gillespie Thomas E Dr (03 05 09)
207	Bromley John J (03 05 43)
208	Slattery John (03 05 45)
209	Dalton Vincent (03 05 46)
210	Lennon James (03 05 49)
211	McHenry Desmond P (03 06 00)
212	Kearns Sean Joseph (03 06 04)
213	Murphy Gerard (03 06 07)
214	Meyler Sean Patrick (03 06 10)
215	Casey Dan (03 06 11)
216	Rothery Eoin (03 06 18)
217	Fleming Stephens A (03 06 21)
218	Whelan John (03 06 22)
219	Gallagher Dominic S (03 06 28)
220	Kenny Frank (03 06 42)
221	McNamara Michael (03 06 43)
222	Wright John J (03 06 57)
223	Massey Thomas Anthony (03 06 59)
224	McCann Bernard (03 07 00)
225	McSweeney Larry (03 07 03)
226	O'Brien Michael M (03 07 08)
227	Cunnane Desmond (03 07 16)
228	Ryan Patrick (03 07 21)
229	Dunne Seamus (03 07 28)
230	Beatty Thomas (03 07 29)
231	Long Finbarr (03 07 39)
232	Grogan James P (03 07 45)
233	Reid Daniel (03 07 50)
234	Eakin Terry (03 07 51)
235	Gaffney Edward (03 07 54)
236	Grant Glenn Gilbert (03 08 08)
237	Winterlich Edward (03 08 11)
238	Bennett Clifford C (03 08 25)
239	McGuire John (03 08 36)
240	Murtagh Vincent P (03 08 40)
241	Burke Patrick J (03 08 45)
242	Doyle Peter (03 08 46)
243	Richardson Gerard (03 09 07)
244	Matthews Niall (03 09 09)
245	Kavanagh James Eugene (03 09 11)
246	Buckley Patrick (03 09 27)
247	O'Connor Thomas (03 09 29)
248	O'Sullivan Jeremiah T (03 09 30)
249	Walsh Declan (03 09 33)
250	Donnelly Patrick J (03 09 48)
251	Daniel Jack (03 09 52)
252	Forde Denis (03 09 54)
253	Sweeney Ernest (03 09 55)
254	Carroll Noel (03 09 56)
255	Campbell Jonathan G (03 10 02)

want to give him any publicity.' The incident was redolent of the infamous moment in the closing stages of the Olympic Marathon in Athens in 2004 when the then leader Vanderlei Cordeiro de Lima was halted and grappled by spectator Neil Horan, an Irish priest, who was later defrocked. The Brazilian ultimately finished third.

May went on to have a stellar marathon career beginning with a maiden National Marathon Championship win in 1981. She finished eighteenth in the marathon at the European Championships in Athens in 1982; thirteenth at the World Championships in Helsinki in 1983 and twenty-eighth in the inaugural women's Olympic Marathon at the Los Angeles Games in 1984.

She developed a love affair with Japan, twice winning the Osaka Marathon, setting another new Irish women's marathon record of 2:28.07 in the 1985 race which stood for twelve years.

Clonliffe Harriers' Mary Walsh finished second (3:02.27) in the women's race, just ahead of Brenda Hon, a member of the Dallas-based Metroplex Strikers Track Club in the US. There were high-profile casualties in the women's race, among them a future winner, Emily Dowling and Mary Butler, who together with her sister Denise and journalist Lindie Naughton operated the women's registration desk in Kevin Street College of Technology the previous day.

'Looking back, I should never have started for three reasons: I was on the committee, I'd only run a marathon in August and I was injured in September. I dropped out in Raheny and got a lift back to the finish to see Carey being presented with her trophy,' said Butler who finished ninth the following year in 3.12.

Christopher A. Dolly was officially the last of the 1,421 runners to cross the finish line in 6:06.12. The real story is more interesting. Better known as Gus to his colleagues in Blackrock AC and his friends in the Stillorgan branch of Slender Health, he was in bed recovering from flu on Marathon Monday. However, he lent his race number to a club colleague's friend.

Imagine his surprise when an RTE journalist rang the following morning to discuss his performance. He carried off the interview with aplomb. He learned from the reporter what time his colleague's friend had done and promised he would be back to break three hours the following year.

Future Labour party leader Ruairi Quinn (4:49.54), Radio 2 DJ Jimmy Greeley (4:36.04) and journalist Vincent Browne (5:18.54) were among the finishers as were the BHAA Chairman Alex Sweeney (2:44.33), the high-ranking BLE official Eddie Spillane (2:43.06)

and two founder members of the BHAA Bertie Messitt (2:54.45) and Dominic Branigan (3:27.44).

Mary Cherry and her parents Maire and David from Dublin ran together and crossed the line within three seconds of each other in four hours and forty-three seconds.

An apocryphal story is told of a runner who stopped outside Connolly Station seemingly exhausted with six miles still to go. A woman emerged from a nearby pub and thrust a glass of brandy into his hand. The grateful runner gulped down the drink. Revived, he broke into

a jog and finished the race. Only then did he realise he had broken his pioneer pledge and drank alcohol for the first time.

A Chicago doctor William Speers described the event as 'the friendliest marathon' and for years afterwards the event was marketed as the 'Friendly Marathon.'

In keeping with the BHAA tradition, all finishers were offered refreshments afterwards in Kevin Street College of Technology. There was one snag, however, as Mary Butler, who went back to assist with the catering, recalls. The canteen was on the top floor.

'Either there was no lift or we'd no access to it, so all the poor marathon runners had to climb four or five flights of stairs after their run to get their drinks and snacks.'

The feel good factor generated by the event was reflected in a letter published afterwards in the *Irish Times*. Ian Kennedy from Stranmillis, Belfast wrote: 'Sir, On this day of gloom in Ireland with the beginning of the hunger strikes in the H-Blocks, I feel it is worth mentioning a great event which took place in Dublin this afternoon (October 27) which surely demonstrated that the people from all parts of Ireland can do something together and get great enjoyment out of it.

'I refer to the Dublin City Marathon which I ran just a couple of hours ago. The reception from the people of Dublin at every street corner was magnificent. All contestants were applauded and offered water at official and unofficial water stations. The Garda cleared the way for all the two thousand entrants and gave encouragement themselves. I ran for a while with a man from Cork, and the crack was good. Others asked me could they tag along and the last thing on their minds was what kind of Irishman I was. The main thing was to finish the course and the last two hundred yards into the finish was like winning the World Cup.

'Surely we should ask some of the politicians who are at loggerheads on both sides of the border to run in next year's marathon and perhaps they will see that we are all the same. This is an occasion when politics can be brought into sport with no sinister undertones.

'Having finished the marathon in some distress, the words of John Robb in last week's *Irish Times* came to what was left of my mind. "There can be no doubt that it is better to chase life rather than death." By surviving the marathon I'm sure over a thousand others would agree that it's great to be alive.

'When the sportsmen and sportswomen of Ireland on this and countless other occasions come together there must be hope for the future,' he wrote.

The people of Dublin – including the Taoiseach Charles Haughey – enthusiastically embraced the event. The unique atmosphere on the first marathon Monday was captured by journalist Niall Kiely, who ran the event, in the *Irish Times* the next day.

'Admiring Dublin opened its generous arms yesterday afternoon and clasped two thousand footsore triers to its bosom, having clapped, and chided and generally chivvied most of them around a meandering run of 26 miles and 385 long yards over the city's streets and suburban road. And at the end of the day the hugely enthusiastic crowds, the heady elixir of applause and the runners' unutterable pleasure at reaching the finishing line had combined to make the first-ever Dublin City Marathon a roaring success.'

And he concluded;

'I saw Charlie Haughey, never a man to miss a good opportunity, out in his old stomping ground in Donnycarney, dressed casually in slacks and pullover. I hadn't time to stop and talk to him, but if I had I would have given him a bit of sound advice: Why doesn't he nationalise the Dublin City Marathon? It's doing more good for the image of this country than ten Knock airports.'

For the marathon (and the airport) the best was yet to come.

Copy

62 St. Brendan's Ave.,
St. Brendan's Estate,
Coolock,
Dublin 5.
2-11-82.

Dear Father O'Donnell,

Thank you for your letter dated 2nd November. Let me straight away apologise for the delay in replying to you, I was sick for the past 3 weeks with a bad chest infection but thank God I'M on the mend again. However I'm back in harness again and will try as best as I can to answer the different points raised in your letter.

1.

Re/Certificate of Approval. We had gone to great lengths at a meeting prior to the 1981 Dublin City Marathon and received subsequently what was agreed between us.- a Certificate of Approval of the event on behalf of B.L.E. athletes so that they could compete in same. Obviously B.L.E. have had second thoughts on the above agreement and this year supplied us with a permit. If B.L.E. had fears about their original agreement they should have contacted the B.H.A.A. and discussed the change.No doubt we will have further talks on this subject in the coming year.

2.

We agree (as we always have) to meet and coordinate our events, but we did not agree at the meeting that in the event of a clash of fixtures that could not be resolved, that the decision of the Competition Sec. of the BLE would be accepted. We can however discuss this particular point at our first fixtures meeting whenever it is called.

3.

We are prepared to discuss our team format and date for next years B.H.A.A. Track and Field Championships.

4.

Agreed.

One final point I would like to make and that is to express my disappointment at the manner in which BLE have handed out suspensions to athletes concerning our Track and Field competition held 4th September. In my own case it seems that my suspension was handed out because I officiated

Chapter 5

A Running Row

Correspondence between the BHAA and the BLE, 1982.

In the twenty-first century big-city marathons are essentially celebratory, inclusive events designed to showcase the host city to both participants and spectators. The health benefits of running are now established beyond doubt as are the economic spin-offs.

Dr Paul Hanly from the National College of Ireland's School of Business estimated that the 2016 Dublin Marathon contributed at least €14.6m to Dublin's economy, which is the equivalent of 127 full-time jobs. But this wasn't always the case and the fledgling Dublin City Marathon came perilously close to being a victim of a long-time schism in Irish athletics.

In the early years of the world-wide marathon boom, the mainstream athletic organisations were painfully slow to recognise their sport was experiencing a revolution. They stuck rigidly to their doctrine that the ordinary man – and particular woman – had no place in a marathon and that the fun-run fad would pass. Indeed, before the first Dublin Marathon, *Irish Times* journalist Niall Kiely wrote that running a marathon smacked of 'dangerous, and perhaps for some even terminal, lunacy.'

The vacuum was filled by others. The New York Marathon was organised by the New York Road Runners' Club, which was effectively controlled by Fred Lebow, while the London Marathon was founded by Olympians, Chris Brasher, a journalist with the *Observer* newspaper at the time, and John Disley.

So it ought not to have been particularly noteworthy that the Dublin City Marathon was not organised by BLE, then the primary governing body for athletics in Ireland. What distinguished the Dublin Marathon from the other big-city marathons, however, were the difficulties between BLE and the organisers, the BHAA.

Without fail every September between 1981 and 1983 the row would spill into the public domain. The athletic press was more sympathetic to the BLE case, but they had a formidable foe in Noel Carroll, who was the public face of the Dublin Marathon. He was an able debater and because of his distinguished career in athletics his views on the sport were universally respected.

The success of the Dublin Marathon caught BLE by surprise. Though they never acknowledged it publicly, they regretted the fact that they had no control over the highest-profile athletic event in the country. But the row had its origins in the split that had festered in Irish athletics for more than half a century and worsened after a failed effort in 1967 to unite the various factions under a new umbrella organisation.

'BLE reacted very badly to the arrival of the BHAA onto the running scene. They were afraid of these people invading their sport,' suggests Dick Hooper, who unwittingly became a central figure in the dispute that unfolded after the launch of the Dublin Marathon.

For the most part though, these squabbles happened under the radar and didn't generate any press coverage. There was no hint for example, of the ongoing hostilities between the two organisations prior to the first Dublin Marathon in 1980. All that changed two months later.

At the annual BLE Congress in Sligo, delegates backed a motion proposed by a future President of the organisation, Padraig Griffin, which essentially instructed the association to examine the participation of its registered athletes in non-sanctioned races including the Dublin City Marathon.

The following April BLE issued a stark warning to its members: 'Registered members of BLE may compete only in events for which a BLE permit has been issued.'

Dick Hooper ignored the directive taking part in a BHAA race ahead of his planned defence of his BLE National Marathon title in Cork later that month. Noel Carroll also competed, as did a number of other BLE runners.

Hooper believes his innate stubbornness, allied to the support of Carroll, enabled him essentially to risk his career. 'I probably didn't take it as seriously as I should have. I was kinda bull headed about it. I just couldn't contemplate the idea of them suspending me.

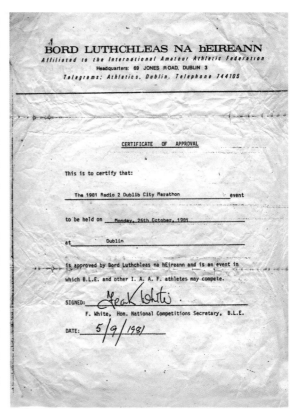

Above: BLE approval for the running of the 1982 Dublin Marathon.

Opposite: A newspaper cutting discussing the field in the men's race in the 1981 marathon, and mentioning the sacroiliac strain that kept Dick Hooper out of the race.

'BLE knew they were losing the public relations battle. They were unsure of what kind of reaction they would get if they actually suspended anybody. They threatened all the time, but were afraid to follow through.

'Noel Carroll carried serious weight; he was a BLE man, but he saw the value of having the BHAA involved. He was always on the airwaves and his views carried serious clout,' said Hooper who subsequently won his third National Marathon in a row in Cork in 1981.

Despite talks behind the scenes the ongoing row escalated again in late August just five days before the closing date for entries to the 1981 marathon. By then an astonishing 7,500 – a threefold increase on the 1980 figure – had applied to run. A banner headline on the front page of the *Evening Herald* on August 21 summed up the story '*Hands off the marathon*, say angry athletes.'

'I'm definitely running regardless,' declared Hooper. 'One thing I don't like is that threat. The word "suspension" seems to be very popular at present, but to me it seems a very childish attitude towards a race which has become a phenomenon.'

In the end, a formula acceptable to the two organisations was agreed upon and the threat of runners being suspended for taking part was lifted. Ironically, Hooper didn't make it to the line. A sacroiliac strain ruled him out of the race.

Right on cue the row erupted again in the autumn of 1982. A decision by the BHAA to organise a track and field championship infuriated BLE. Still, even though relations between the two bodies were at an all-time low it wasn't in the interests of either party to endanger the marathon. But it was another close-run thing.

Frank Greally, editor of the newly launched *Irish Runner*, was now an increasingly influential figure in Irish athletics. In an editorial published in the pre-race edition of the magazine he wrote, 'There is no doubt but that a governing body such as BLE must have some form of control and commitment from their affiliated athletes, but the governing body should also have a duty to give the athletes in question a fair hearing without just simply passing down suspensions and making this fact public even before the athletes in question are aware of it themselves.'

Another eleventh-hour agreement was hammered out that enabled BLE athletes to compete. Behind the scenes though, the pressure was been ramped up on the organisers. Louis Hogan recalls being summoned to a meeting with the RTE

Committee members pictured outside the Mansion House.

[Pic. Brian Tansey]

RACE MAKERS

Above: Ballyhaunis native Michael Joyce sporting an *Irish Runner* singlet.

THE marathon is a great sporting event. It's long and hard, but it's enjoyable for those who are prepared for it and it's one of the best sports happenings in Ireland today. And on a world scale it can measure up to the best in every way.

The Radio 2 Dublin city marathon just doesn't happen. Nearly 11,000 runners don't just turn up on the long week-end at the end of October and head off around the roads and streets of the capital without some sort of guidance.

No, behind the scenes there is a dynamic organising committee. A team of loyal and dedicated workers, who, in their own way, are as fit for the task they undertake as are those runners who break the three-hour marathon barrier. And that takes a bit of doing.

To say a million-and-one things have to be done before the starting gun is fired for the Radio 2 Dublin city marathon is not far short of the mark. There are literally thousands of things to be looked after, including the receipt and processing of all entry forms.

Under the shrewd guidance of chairman Ciaran Looney, the organising committee have perfected the organising of the great Dublin event and each year they drive themselves towards even higher goals, if that is possible.

The real excitement and enthusiasm of the marathon hits the runners on the acutal day of the race. But the people behind the scenes are affected much earlier. Their work begins in January each year, and in the nine months up to the big day they work feverishly – all in a voluntary capacity – to make sure everything goes like clockwork.

"The proof of the pudding is in the eating", and so it is with this race. Anyone who has participated in it will only rave about it. The excitement. The wit of the Dublin people en route. The carnival atmosphere of the whole thing. The way it is organised. If a prize was to be awarded each year for the best organised sporting event in this country, it surely would have to be shared equally by the true-blues who make

Page 18

up the marathon organising committee.

The Dublin marathon has become so big now the 'Committee had to acquire an office to cater for the workload. The organisers work through the Winter, and an awful lot of the effort is done in their own time. Which means their leisure time is cut back, and drastically reduced as the big day approaches.

For some, lunch-time is even utilised to get this little job, or that little job complete. There is no double time for night duty either. But it's all a labour of love, and the reward for these people is seeing the smiles of satisfaction when the finishers collect their plaques at the end of the gruelling 26-mile course.

MEET THE PEOPLE

Chairman is **Ciaran Looney**, who holds a similar post with the association that oversees the event, the B.H.A.A. He is an experienced administrator. There are few bigger-hearted workers for athletics in the country.

Kilkennyman **Ned Sweeney** works in the administrative end. A man of boundless enthusiasm, he used to enjoy running himself but willingly cut back on it to concentrate on working behind the scenes for the marathon.

Regisration and work at the finish is looked after by **Dominic Branigan.** No one needs reminding of the importance of this work. No better man than Dominic to keep a cool head and have everything in tip-top shape.

Zia Whyte is the ladies' co-ordinator. She is deeply involved in marathon affairs and is an invaluable member of the team.

Results and timing are the responsibility of **Cathal Convery.** His duty is to ensure there is no foul-up in this important sector. Every finisher, be he near the back or front, likes to know his time and place. You can thank Cathal for this. With nearly 11,000 in the field you can gauge the enormity of this task.

Brian Higgins looks after security. When the runners are sweating it out around the course, Brian makes sure their gear is safe and well protected. His job is to organise the

team to do this job properly.

Jimmy Naughton sees each entrant has a special Radio-2 bag to hold their gear while they are away. They must be on hand at all times and easily accessible. Then they must be deposited properly so each runner will have the minimum of trouble retrieving them when they finish.

To make sure each finisher gets a bronze plaque is the task entrusted to **Marian O'Connell.** Again proper advance planning is the key. Marian has it all down to a fine art.

Course director is **Alex Sweeney** and with this 26 miles' long race you can imagine the workload involved. Before the race he has to examine this in detail and iron out any likely trouble spots.

Everyone knows about the Radio-2 Dublin Marathon. That is the biggest compliment that can be paid to P.R.O. **Noel Carroll.** He has managed to make it one of the best publicised events in the world.

The key responsibility at the start and finish is thrust on **Billy Kennedy.** His job is to make sure the race starts on time and there are no hitches when the tired athletes return home.

To make sure the feed stations are properly manned and stocked is the job of **Marion Kavanagh.** Thousands of cups and sponges, and gallons of water and other drinks must be acquired here. Like a mother catering for a big family, Marian sees to it all.

Those unfortunate runners who in the past have had to drop out for one reason or another didn't catch the bus back home. They got a lift, and this was thanks to the work of **Mary Higgins.** Transport is the task thrown into her lap.

The B.H.A.A. committee for 1983 is: Ciaran Looney (chairman), Frank Slevin (Vice-chairman), Annette Croke (secretary), Marian Kavanagh (assistant-secretary), Dominic Branigan (registrar), Billy Kennedy (treasurer), Noel Carroll, Jimmy Naughton, Marian O'Connell, Pat O'Grady, Alex Sweeney, Ned Sweeney and Zia Whyte.

Official Race Programme 1983.

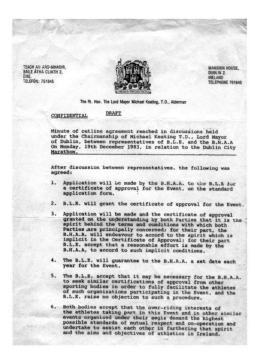

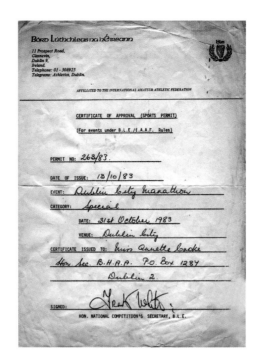

Director-General Vincent Finn. 'You've got me into another fine mess,' Finn suggested to Hogan before going on to explain that he had just had a call from the private secretary of the Taoiseach Charles Haughey.

It had been put to the Taoiseach that BLE should take over the running of the marathon. 'I explained the philosophy of the event and how inclusive the race was. I suggested that if BLE were allowed to take it over this would no longer be the case. I urged the DG to hold the line.' Hogan never heard any more about the matter.

But like a scene from the movie *Groundhog Day*, the entire controversy was played out again in the run-up to the 1983 race. As usual a last-minute settlement was hammered out between the parties. Ultimately, under the auspices of the Lord Mayor of Dublin and junior minister with responsibility for sport, Michael Keating, a binding agreement was reached between the warring parties in December 1993. Essentially the six-clause agreement gave the BHAA the right to continue to run the marathon for everyone so long as they applied for a certificate of approval from BLE.

The BHAA had won the war, though the magnanimity of BLE needs to be acknowledged as well. Within a decade they had designated the event as their National championship. But the inescapable fact is that BLE never capitalised on the first running boom. 'It could have been BLE who made serious money out of it, but they missed the boat,' says Dick Hooper.

Billy Kennedy (left) and Alex Sweeney discuss options after a technical hitch knocks out their PA system.

Dick Hooper on his way to his second Dublin Marathon win, in a time of 2:13.47, in 1985.

Chapter 6

The Marathon Goes Mainstream

Emily Dowling on her way to winning the 1981 Dublin Marathon. In the background (on top of the van), Neil Cusack, winner of the men's race, cheers her home.

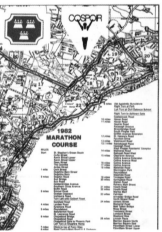

Running came in from the cold in Ireland after the first Dublin Marathon. Noel Carroll noted the change in '*The Runner's Book*' which was published in 1981. He wrote: 'I used to be an eccentric: now I'm an expert. I was once tolerated: now I'm consulted. I have graduated from being somebody who should know better to somebody who knows better.'

The unthinkable had happened. The marathon had become accessible to the ordinary man and woman. The legendary Czechoslovakian distance runner Emil Zátopek once said, 'If you want to run, run a mile. If you want to experience a different life, run a marathon.' And that's what thousands of Irish people did in the first half of the 1980s.

There was another reason, though, for the growth in the popularity of marathons. Ireland was in the depths of an economic recession. Unemployment and inflation were rampant.

According to the Central Statistics Office, real average earnings fell by 4.5 per cent between 1980 and 1982 due to high inflation. People had extra time on their hands and running was an affordable and enjoyable form of recreation.

Completing a marathon became an achievable goal giving people a sense of purpose in an otherwise bleak environment. This phenomenon was repeated after the Celtic Tiger imploded when there was another spike in the numbers taking up running.

We moved to Raheny in 1981 and within a few months dad joined Raheny Shamrock Athletic Club, which was to play a huge role in his life. The photo was taken by my mother, Nora Lynam, at the top of our road (Lough Derg Road) in Raheny. Dad always said the enthusiastic home support in Raheny kept his spirits up at the difficult 20-mile mark. There was always a huge cheer any time a green t-shirt (The Shamrock colours) was spotted coming around the corner. The plastic flask cup and my dodgy fringe place the photo firmly in the 80's!

Jackie Lynam

Tommy Lynam with his daughter Jackie.

Dublin Marathon (circa 1983/84)

The boom caught everybody by surprise, including the organisers of the Dublin Marathon. Shortly after he won the inaugural race in 1980 Dick Hooper forecast that five thousand would run in 1981. The general expectation was a maximum of four thousand entries. A total of 8,257 entered and 6,817 started the race, which began an hour earlier than the previous year on a significantly altered course.

Meantime, members of the marathon committee continued to fine tune their organisational skills. Billy Kennedy and Brian Price ran in the inaugural London Marathon in 1981. 'Until I hit the wall at twenty miles, I clearly saw the organisation at the start, along the route and the finish,' remembers Price.

Together with Ned Sweeney, they were given access to the finish area to observe how the organisers coped with recording the finishing placings and times of 6,255 runners. They also cemented their links with London marathon founders, Chris Brasher – who had visited Dublin to see the inaugural Radio 2 Marathon in 1980 – and John Disley. Price also made contact with Fred Lebow while on a trip to New York and the pair struck up a lasting friendship

The phenomenal growth in the Dublin event was highlighted again when the 1982 marathon attracted 11,076 entries, making it the fourth-biggest marathon in the world after London, New York and Honolulu.

But success brought its own unique set of challenges. Aside from the ongoing battles with BLE, the marathon – contrary to popular belief – was struggling financially, even though the entry fee had increased from £1.50 to £5 in 1981.

A detailed breakdown of the marathon finances was published in the 1982 race programme. It made sobering reading – particularly the revelation that if the participants had to meet the full cost of the race the entry fee would be £20.

'The reason that they don't pay so much is because so many people work for nothing, many public services are laid on free and much support is forthcoming from commercial concerns,' noted the unnamed author of the article.

The list of sponsors had grown exponentially since 1980. Seiko, who provided the clocks for the first marathon, were now one of the main sponsors supplying all the timing equipment free of charge. Hertz and Smurfit Computing remained involved as well.

In addition, shoe manufacturing companies Puma, Nike, Brooks and New Balance were backing the event as were Marathon Bars, Sno Yogurt, Volvic, Erin Food, Roma Foods, Motorola, Aer Lingus, Dublin Tourism, AnCo, Brook Bond Oxo, Tele Communications Ltd, Data General, Gowan Motors and Vita Cortex – who supplied sponges. These were soaked in water and runners used them to cool down.

According to the programme the £5 entry fee was used to meet the following expenses: Finishers' plaque £2; Insurance, telephones, security and signage £1; Electrical equipment, portacabins and portaloos £1; Entry forms and stationery 80p and miscellaneous expenses 20p.

The cost of the feeding stations on the race route were primarily met by XLI Medisport – a sports drink manufacturer – and gear and shoe company Adidas. Cospóir sponsored the race numbers which were made by clients in the Central Remedial Clinic in Clontarf, while Dublin Corporation gave a grant of £1,000.

The Corporation didn't charge for the other services they provided and neither did the Gardaí, the Office of Public Works, the Defence Forces, Dublin Tourism, the Civil Defence and St John's ambulance. All the promotional costs, which RTE Controller of Programmes Billy Wall estimated to be worth between forty and fifty thousand pound, were met by the station. Nowadays, the promotional costs are met by the organising committee in association with the sponsors.

Other than the previous race winners, all entrants – including members of the race committee – had to pay the entrance fee. RTE sponsored a Dublin Crystal trophy for the first man and woman home. No appearance fees or expenses were paid to either officials or runners.

Peter Rogan Recalls How Seán Boylan Saved His Marathon

Having completed my training for the 1982 Dublin Marathon (my second),I was really looking forward to the big day. However, on the Saturday morning before the Marathon, I woke early with severe cramps on both legs. I spent all day Saturday resting and massaging my legs, hoping that the cramps would go. Sunday morning was worse, however, and I had more or less abandoned hope of being able to compete, as I could barely move.

My next-door neighbour Ultan (a great GAA man) called to wish me good luck. When I told him how I was, he suggested bringing me to Kingscourt where Meath were playing Cavan that afternoon. To quote Ultan, 'Meath have a new manager. I don't know what he's like at the football, but they say he's great with the cures. I'll ask him to have a look at you.' I agreed.

After the match I was taken into the dressing room where Seán Boylan, the new Meath manager, worked on my legs for a while, then stunned me, saying that on my way to the marathon to divert around to Bettystown beach – thirty miles from home – and walk in the sea for fifteen minutes.

I was very sceptical of this idea, but decided that I had nothing to lose. So, at 7.30 am on marathon morning, I was at Bettystown wading thigh-high into the ice-cold sea while my young children were rolling around on the sands in fits of laughter at their mad dad.

I had the last laugh. Shortly after setting off from Bettystown, I could find the cramps easing. By the time I got to the start, I didn't even have a twinge and ran a very comfortable marathon.

Fast forward five years to 1987. Meath were now All-Ireland champions. Seán Boylan was on his way to becoming a GAA legend. But on the Bank Holiday Monday in 1982, he was my miracle man.

The total income for the 1981 marathon was £36,000 while expenditure was £33,000 leaving a surplus of £3,000 which was carried forward to the 1982 race.

'Showing a slight surplus is part of the organising committee's policy. This marathon should not lose money and it is good business to come out slightly ahead and put the event on a sound footing for future years. After all the marathon is run by the Business Houses Athletic Association,' said the programme note writer.

Such was the thirst for information among marathoners that official clinics, sponsored by Gowan Motors were held in the company's showrooms during the summer months of 1981 and 1982.

Dick Hooper headed an expert panel which included fellow marathoners Emily Dowling, Mary Purcell and Noel Carroll. Other panellists were physiotherapists Amy Johnson, whose clients included the all-conquering Kerry football team, and Siobhan Treacy, whose daughter Sara competed in the Rio Olympics in 2016.

The late Dr Risteard Mulcahy provided medical expertise, while Anne Barry of the Irish Heart Foundation gave dietary information. Members of the marathon's organising committee also attended. The success of the clinics can be gauged from the attendance of over 1,500 runners in 1981.

Noel Carroll's slots on RTE 2's *Drivetime* show on Monday evenings were the primary source of information for runners outside Dublin and when local radio became more established Alex Sweeney provided expert advice to their listeners. In addition *The RTE Guide*, the Irish Runner magazine – which first appeared in 1980 – and *Magill* magazine all published training schedules for participants. Vincent Browne, the founder and then editor of *Magill* participated in the first two Dublin City Marathons.

'I did a lot of training for the 1980 race, but then got injured. I decided I needed to do a long run a week before the race. I wore a new pair of shoes and my feet badly blistered. After six miles I struggled in the race. The next year I did less training, but had no problems in the race itself. I decided to retire on that note,' recalls Browne.

The involvement of Smurfit Computer in compiling the results provided the organisers with additional valuable statistical information. This was summarised by results co-ordinator Ned Sweeney in a foreword to the official results booklet which was mailed to every finisher a couple of weeks after the race.

The stand-out statistics from the 1981 race were that 95 per cent of the starting field finished, while 82 per cent of the entrants started the race. 'This [start rate] was surprisingly

Left: Peter Rogan in Clontarf during the 1981 Dublin Marathon.
Centre: The Rogan family on Bettystown Beach.
Right: Peter Rogan running the 2004 Dublin Marathon.

low compared to other major marathons in the US and Europe and suggests that many aspirants found the necessary preparation beyond them for one reason or another,' wrote Sweeney, who described the 95 per cent finishing rate as a truly remarkable achievement.

By way of comparison 78 per cent of the entrants in the 2018 race finished. But the number of entrants was more than three times bigger – 20,963 compared to 6,817 in 1981.

In the early days, finishing times were only recorded at thirty second intervals. Smurfit Computing wrote an extrapolation program to create random finish times between the timed ones. This only partially solved the issue as no account was taken of how long it took runners to cross the start line. Nowadays chip timing is the norm; back in the eighties chips were what you ate after the race!

Conor Faughnan, director of Consumer Affairs for AA Ireland, ruefully discovered this anomaly when he competed in the 1981 race as a twelve-year-old.

'The crowds were so big that there was thirty minutes on the race clock before I passed under the start gantry. It was another mile or two before the field had thinned to the point where I could actually run. I clocked four hours and twenty-eight minutes. But my time over the ground was probably more like 3.50 which was more in keeping with my training times.'

Dick Hooper's withdrawal due to injury robbed the 1981 marathon of what might have been a classic duel with Neil Cusack, who finished second the previous year. The Limerick man, once hailed as Ireland's potentially best ever long distance runner, was on a mission of redemption in the early 1980s.

After a stellar career at schools' level, he moved to the US in 1969 on an athletic scholarship in East Tennessee State University in Johnson City.

He was the stand-out athlete in what became known as the 'Irish Brigade' in the college, which included the Leddy brothers, PJ and Eddie from Leitrim, Ray McBride (Galway), Kevin Breen (Offaly) and Mayo native Frank Greally, who after his return to Ireland founded *Irish Runner* magazine and is now an ambassador for the 'Daily Mile' an initiative designed

Dick Hooper's advice to competitors in the 1981 Dublin City Marathon

Dick Hooper's advice to competitors in the 1981 Dublin City Marathon –

"Just concentrate on getting to the 15 mile mark and at the same time take in as much as you can along the way. Enjoy the scenery, look at the crowd, pick out faces, chat to the person alongside you, enjoy the feeling of freedom, the atmosphere of the race.

"In that way you will be able to relax. Be patient, don't try and rush to get to the finish, it will come in time. Don't be influenced by people charging past you in the early stages. Be disciplined, be confident.

"At 15 miles your mind will turn automatically to finishing the race. That's when the race really starts. Many of you will be coming to the point in the race which you have never ran before, not even in training. "Don't be afraid to take in the discomfort which you will possibly feel at 18 miles; everyone else is feeling like yourself, most even worse. That's the discovery of the Marathon. Discovery of yourself. And enjoy the elation of coming into the finish, gliding those last few hundred yards. A moment to cherish."

Taking Fluids during the race – "You have to take fluids early, even before the race starts. The object is to avoid dehydration and the body is better able to absorb fluid in the early stages of the marathon.

If you want your own special drinks at the feeding stations then arrange to have them delivered. It can often be very helpful but ordinary water can fill the bill although most of the top marathon runners in the world have their own opinions about what suits them best.

"Other runners use a special diet during the week leading up to the marathon which they feel brings them through the "wall" at 18 to 20 miles. Personally I've never bothered with any special diet and feel that solid eating habits are sufficient."

Gear – "If the day is reasonably good, not terribly cold, then a vest is sufficient; if it's really cold, like a winter's day then it can be advisable to wear a T-shirt under your vest but when you start to sweat this can become very heavy.

"As regards shoes – wear those you are used to and have broken in well during training. Make sure the heels are straight and not worn down on the edges.

"Good Luck".
And the same to you Dick.

to improve the fitness and well-being of primary school children in Ireland.

Cusack set an Irish 10,000m record at the Munich Olympics in 1972. Later that year, he beat the Olympic marathon champion Frank Shorter to win the US cross country championship in Chicago. However, he was later relegated to fourth place after a steward misdirected him in driving snow near the finish.

But it was his sensational winning performance in the 1974 Boston Marathon at the age of twenty-two that stuck in the public psyche. Money was scarce in the early 1970s and none of the Irish students in ETSU could afford to travel home for Christmas. 'Five of us got together one Christmas with a Presbyterian Minister and headed down to Atlanta to run a marathon for the craic.'

The Peach Bowl Marathon on 18 December 1971 had 101 starters. The night before the race the students wrote down their predicted times. 'When the other lads saw I had put down 2:18 they just laughed. Anyway, the next day I won the marathon in 2:16.18 even though I had turned back a few times for Eddie Leddy. Remember we were only running it for fun. It was a world record time for my age.'

Cusack was twelve days shy of his twentieth birthday. The organisers presented him with a watch. 'From then on I knew I was capable of running a fast marathon.'

Before the start of the 1974 Boston Marathon, Cusack was warming-up in a gym when

Start of the first wheelchair race in 1981: Front row l to r Gerry O'Reilly (Dublin), H Pierce (Clare), Kevin Breen (Dublin). Back row (l to r) Dolores Pierce (Clare), Dean Buckley (Cork)

he was approached by Liscannor native Pat McMahon. He was ten years older than Cusack and had a formidable marathon CV. Twelfth in the Olympic Marathon in 1968; he was third behind Ron Hill in the 1970 Boston Marathon and finished second the following year, just five seconds adrift of the winner Alvaro Mejia.

He asked the tanned student sporting a Phil Lynott hairstyle how he thought he would do. 'I think I could win it,' said Cusack much to the astonishment of McMahon. And he did exactly that in 2:13.40, fifty-six seconds ahead of second placed Tom Fleming. 'Actually it wasn't until I crossed the line that I realised the event was so big,' he admits.

Nowadays, victory in the Boston Marathon would guarantee instant stardom. Unfortunately there was no prize money in those days. 'I did get a few hundred dollars afterwards in appearance fees at road races. And when you're a student everything helps.'

Once he returned to Ireland he faced a different challenge – he had to earn a living. There were no support structures for elite athletes at the time. 'I was back to reality after being virtually a full-time professional athlete. I had to paddle my own canoe.'

Even though he competed in the Montreal Olympic Marathon he found it almost impossible to combine the level of training required with working full-time in a bar. When Limerick hosted the World cross country championships in 1979 he was no longer an elite athlete.

The Dublin Marathon gave him a second chance. 'It was the event which motivated me to get going again. But I knew I needed two years' training before I would be in shape to run something like 2:13.' That moment arrived in the 1981 Dublin Marathon.

'I felt comfortable all the way. I went through ten miles in something like forty-nine

Back in the 80s, we didn't have gels or energy drinks or anything like that. I remember I was coming down towards Fairview and I saw a little girl holding out some glucose sweets. She was right out in the road and looked delighted with herself, so I took one – just so as not to pass her by. A mile or so later I began to really hit the wall – when I remembered the sweet in my hand. I stuck it in my mouth and sucked it – and I felt I got a real boost that carried me through to the finish. I don't know whether it was all in my head or if it really did help, but I've never forgotten it!
Stephen Carr, Dublin Marathon 1983

Matt Shields (above, in red t-shirt) running in the first ever parkrun event in the Republic of Ireland, Malahide Castle and Gardens, November 2012.

minutes and I remember Dick Hooper, who was doing the radio commentary, saying he felt sorry for me because he didn't think I could last the pace.'

By halfway he was racing solo and looking on course to challenge Louis Kenny's Irish record time of 2:12.21. Although he slowed slightly over the final three miles he still cruised home in 2:13.58, eighteen seconds slower than his winning time in Boston seven years previously.

Northern Ireland's Greg Hannon was second exactly three minutes behind Cusack with Mick Byrne (2:18.08) and Pat Hooper (2:20.1) third and fourth respectively. Matt Shields, who later was instrumental in introducing the phenomenally popular parkruns in Ireland, was fifth.

The women's race was much more competitive despite the absence of the defending champion Carey May who had moved to study and train in Utah. Emily Dowling made up for the disappointment of having to drop out of her first two marathons by taking the women's

Wheelchair participants before the off.

title in 2:48.22, seventy-eight seconds clear of her Dublin City Harriers team mates Deirdre Nagle (2:49.40) and Greta Hickey (2:53.13).

There were eight competitors in the inaugural wheelchair section with Michael Cunningham first over the line. It was an important breakthrough for para-athletes because they were not allowed compete in either the New York or London Marathons up until then. The previous year Jim Gallagher was the first visually impaired athlete to complete a marathon. Alex Sweeney wanted an open policy from day one. 'As far as I was concerned the runner who finished last was just as important as the race winner and above all I wanted the race to be inclusive.'

The first meeting of the organising committee for the 1982 Dublin City Marathon took place on 25 March 1982, six months ahead of the race. The entries poured in during the subsequent months. Of the record 11,076 who entered the race, 9,075 registered in the Mansion House and only 125 of those failed to make it to the finish.

Neil Cusack was back to defend his title while Dick Hooper, who had never been beaten

Dublin Marathon
Commitee member
John O'Reilly with
Minister of State,
Michael Keating, before
the marathon in 1981.

on Irish soil in the marathon, toed the line just six weeks after finishing a creditable eleventh in the European Championship Marathon in Athens. The joker in the pack was Listowel born-Dublin based school-teacher, Jerry Kiernan who was making his debut over the classic distance.

One of the country's most versatile runners, the Clonliffe Harrier athlete initially looked destined for a glittering career on the track. In 1976 he became the seventh Irishman to break four minutes for the mile when he ran 3:59.2 in London. Ultimately though, he switched his focus to road racing. The twenty-nine-year old had been the dominant figure on the scene in the summer of 1982, breaking 46.30 in three different ten-mile races.

He was on schedule for a sensational two-hour, nine minute finish at the fifteen-mile mark on marathon Monday. By twenty miles he had a lead of nearly four minutes. Raheny was the must-be-place to watch the marathon which was being televised live for the first time.

As the runners approached a sharp incline on Station Road near where St Francis Hospice is now situated, they were greeted with a scene which resembled a Tour de France mountain finish as spectators encroached onto the road forcing the runners to negotiate the

hill in single file.

Kiernan was beginning to feel the pain. Tom O'Riordan's graphic race report in *Irish Runner* noted that the Kerryman had stopped momentarily at sixteen miles suffering from cramp. At twenty-two miles he still looked on target to break Louis Kenny's Irish record, but the real drama unfolded in the last four miles when his four-minute lead became very precarious.

'Finally, as Kiernan drew closer to the great hour of glory the hamstrings began to tighten. That coupled with exhaustion and leg weariness left him almost tottering around Merrion Square. There he stopped for the third time and Eamon [Coghlan] came off the timing truck once more to help him,' reported O'Riordan.

He crossed the finish line in 2:13.47 with the second-placed runner Frederik Vandervennet just sixty-seven seconds behind. Irish-American Kevin McCarey was third; Kildare's Paddy Murphy was fourth while Dick Hooper finished fifth. Neil Cusack dropped out.

Twenty-three-year old American Debbie Mueller, who won a trip to the race, promptly won it in 2:40.58. In the wheelchair section Dubliner Gerry O'Rourke began his dominance of the event.

The bravery of Kiernan's performance was the stand-out feature of the race, though it did generate controversy. Marathon doyen Noel Henry, a member of Clonliffe Harriers, in a letter published in the *Irish Runner* was critical of the roles played by David Taylor and Eamon Coghlan in the drama. Taylor, a clubmate of Kiernan, who didn't have a race number did a training run over the first fifteen miles in the lead group. Nowadays, pace-makers are an integral part of big city marathons, but they were still frowned upon back in the early 1980s.

'[The] idea of using the race "as a training run" and then setting a fast pace alongside Jerry

David Taylor runs
alongside Jerry Kiernan
(3044).

Kiernan for thirteen miles at which point he dropped out, undoubtedly had a very unsettling effect on some of Kiernan's rivals.

'Eamon Coghlan's ... behaviour in entering the race at a crucial stage to run alongside a fading Jerry Kiernan has given rise to some considerable comments. No doubt the Belgian visitor, the runner up, would have appreciated similar aid. I do not wish to detract from Jerry Kiernan's magnificent performance, but it is unfair that one runner should benefit from this sort of help when others are prepared to go it alone.

'This ... indicates a lack of respect towards fellow athletes and is resented by many – in short it is not playing the game and should not have been permitted,' wrote Henry.

His comments were echoed by Frank Greally in the magazine's editorial. He suggested that if Kiernan broke the Irish record it would not have been recognised due to Eamon Coghlan's interference.

'The marathon is the supreme test of man against the distance and as in boxing the rule should be... seconds out,' opined Greally. As for the man of the moment, he summed up his feelings when he told Tom O'Riordan. 'I admit I have a new respect for it now.' Kiernan, of course, went on to have a stellar career over the distance highlighted by his magnificent ninth place finish in the Olympic Marathon in Los Angeles in 1984.

By far the greatest ire, however, was reserved for RTE's live coverage of the race, which in the words of Frank Greally 'never lived up to expectations'.

Bigger issues were hurtling down the track for the marathon. By the time the 1983 event came around neither Frank Slevin nor Brian Price were involved. A difference of opinion arose between them and the rest of the committee about their involvement in the newly established Brooks *Evening Press* all-women 10km road race launched in June 1983.

Wheelchair participants before the start of the 1982 marathon. Second from left is the eventual winner Gerry O'Rourke.

Gerry O'Rourke might have found his sporting destiny in soccer, but in September 1979 at the age of sixteen after what he euphemistically describes as a 'tangle with a train' he had to find a different sport through which to channel his competitive instincts.

He spent fifteen months in hospital, initially in Dr Steevens' Hospital – now the headquarters of the Health Services Executive – and later in the National Rehabilitation Hospital in Dun

Laoghaire, following an amputation on both his legs.

He subsequently attended the Irish Wheelchair Association in Clontarf where one of his coaches Carol Hayes suggested he try the marathon. 'At the time the IWA was trying to break down barriers and show the public that people with disabilities could participate in mainstream sport.'

The burgeoning Dublin City Marathon was the perfect event for wheelchair athletes to exhibit their prowess and tenacity. However, O'Rourke's tentative plans to compete in the 1981 marathon had to be put on ice as he didn't have a racing chair.

His work colleagues in the Department of Education came to his aid, organised a whip around and raised the £500 needed to purchase one. Initially Gerry trained by pushing himself to and from work each day – a journey of six miles. But it was his training spins on the hills in the Furry Glen in the Phoenix Park that steeled him for the marathon challenge.

Prior to his accident, O'Rourke was playing with the St Patrick's Athletic schoolboy team; he had captained his schools' team to a Leinster soccer title and was due to travel to Coventry City for a trial. So his competitive instincts were well honed before he took up the marathon. 'I wanted to do well in the race – and win it, to be honest.'

In his debut marathon in 1982 his opportunity came when the lead group of wheelchairs reached a hilly section of the course in Finglas. 'My hill training stood to me, I got a bit of a break and found myself three or four hundred metres ahead. Then my competitive instincts kicked in and I just kept going.'

This breakthrough win marked the beginning of an unprecedented period of dominance for O'Rourke. He won the next five Dublin Marathons as well as the London marathon in 1985.

His unbeaten Dublin run came to an end in 1988 when he finished third, just forty-eight hours after returning home from Korea where he had finished fourth in the Paralympic' Marathon.

He retired after winning his seventh Dublin Marathon in 1990. O'Rourke is justifiably proud of the fact that he was the first athlete across the line when he won many of his seven titles.

'I won't tell a lie. I didn't want anybody to catch me. In the early days there wasn't much media coverage of Paralympic sports. So if you were first over the line you were guaranteed coverage, which was great for the sport.'

It is fair to say that as well as being a champion marathoner, Gerry O'Rourke was a pioneering figure in Paralympic sport in Ireland.

We are happy to bring you the FULL results of the Radio 2 Dublin City Marathon. We have checked these results carefully but we would like to point out that we are not responsible for any possible inaccuracies. We are grateful to Smurfit Computing for supplying us with the results and they have been set for us by Kilkenny People. We apologise for the delay in getting this issue to our readers but this was due to a technical fault on the results section which was completely out of our control.

A MESSAGE FROM RESULTS CO-ORDINATOR NED SWEENEY

On behalf of the Organising Committee I am pleased to present the results of this memorable event. But first some statistics which should be of interest.

A total of 8,257 entries were received. Of these, 6,817 started the race. This figure of 82% was surprisingly low when compared with other Major Marathons in Europe and the USA, and suggests that many aspirants found the necessary preparation beyond them for one reason or another. However, of those who did start, a whopping 95% finished the course, a truly remarkable achievement. This is a tribute to the excellent training programme compiled by Noel Carroll which many adopted and of course the resilience of the runners and the great encouragement provided by the spectators along the Marathon route. By comparison, 91% finished the London Marathon and about 88% completed the recent Pony British Marathon.

The logistics of entry, registration and capture of finish data in mass marathons can best be handled by computer techniques and we were fortunate to secure the free services of Smurfit Computing for this event.

The timing process was based on select times using the latest Seiko electronic devises. This ensures that times for all finishers are accurate to a few seconds even at the peak time of 3 to 4 hours.

From the outset, entrants were advised that numbers were non transferable. This is because the computer will recognise only that name which is assigned on entry. As a result, a problem was caused due to the 7th finisher, Billy Gallagher, wearing number 4929 which had been allocated to Irene Gallagher. This was obviously unintentional but led to the lady featuring in that position in the earliest result. If such a mistake were made down the field it could go undetected, so clearly entrants in similar computerised events have a responsibility to ensure that the correct number is worn.

Those finishers marked with an asterix are wheelchair entrants and 10 minutes should be added to the times shown to allow for their earlier start. Ladies are denoted by heavy type.

These results have been carefully checked and we are satisfied that a very high degree of accuracy has been achieved. Over the coming weeks we will be sending each finisher a certificate showing place and time.

To the many volunteers, who throughout the summer, at registration, and on 26th October gave up their time to get the race on the road I express our Committee's deep gratitude. Without them the event could not have taken place.

They had already established a company which provided timing services to road races. Having witnessed the growth in the number of women competing in the Dublin Marathon (70 to 900) they felt there was a market for a women'-only race in Dublin, similar to the 10km race which Fred Lebow had organised in New York in 1972.

They raised this idea at a meeting of the marathon committee, but it wasn't pursued. 'The committee had their hands full with the marathon,' recalled Bertie Messitt in his biography.

Subsequently, Slevin and Price outlined their plan to Michael Sheridan, a journalist with the *Evening Press*, who forwarded it to the paper's promotion department.

Coincidentally, at the same time Keith Burns, an agent for Brooks shoes was in discussions with Eddie McDonagh, a coach with Dundrum South Dublin AC. Eventually at a meeting of the interested parties in the Mill House in Stillorgan the foundations for the women's race were laid.

Through their company Race Management, Slevin and Price offered to organise the race for a fee. 'We had young families; we were being run ragged and didn't have an arse in our trousers,' said Price.

From its launch the event was an unprecedented success with over nine thousand women taking part in the inaugural race much to the chagrin of Fred Lebow. 'He had seven thousand runners in his race that year which he was claiming was a world record. I phoned him after our race and told him we had beaten his record. He was disgusted,' recalls Price.

Members of the Dublin Marathon committee were not best pleased either, as Messitt outlined in his biography. 'It was bad enough to organise the race behind the committee members' back, as they saw it. But to then bring it under the banner of Dundrum, which was affiliated to BLE, struck the committee as a form of treason.'

Reflecting on it now Slevin is more sanguine about the controversy. 'There was a little bit of a dispute. It should never have happened, but people looked at things differently.'

Nonetheless, the upshot was that the Dublin Marathon lost two of its key personnel. It was probably no more than a coincidence, but in the subsequent decade while the *Evening Press* Mini-Marathon flourished and became the biggest women-only race in the world with a field of forty thousand, the Dublin Marathon experienced turbulent times, which put the race in doubt.

Above: 'On your marks ...' 1983. Jerry Kiernan wears bib no. 0001.

Left: Jerry Kiernan shakes hands with well-wishers, including Mick Hickey (far left) and Stan Woods (partially hidden, second row) on the startline.

Chapter 7

'Not Tonight, Love!'

Even during the heady early years of the marathon the organisers recognised that for the race to become a long-term sustainable event it would have to be marketed abroad. Ireland's population wasn't sufficient to sustain an annual big-city marathon indefinitely.

While the race committee recognised the earning potential of the event if overseas runners came to Dublin every October, the civil authorities were less enthusiastic and securing a budget for such a project proved impossible in the early days.

Brian Price recalls attending a meeting with Dublin Tourism along with Noel Carroll.

'We made a presentation about the potential of the race in terms of boosting tourism earnings and pointed out that Fred Lebow was able to attract two thousand overseas visitors to the New York Marathon. At the end of it all I was speechless when an official asked me how much money we had to spend.'

Despite a lack of resources, the committee still did some marketing abroad. Using his contacts in Aer Lingus, Price persuaded crews who worked the Dublin-Manchester route to hand out flyers for the Dublin race at the registration for the Manchester marathon. 'We also brought in a number of foreign journalists to see the race and their articles appeared in a couple of US publications.'

One of those journalists Hal Straus gave a lyrical description of the 1982 race:

'As the cool, bright afternoon turns into chill dusk, he heads back to his hotel room, looking out over the scattered groaning bodies of St Stephen's Green, reminiscent of the battlefield scene in *Gone with the Wind*. The race had been like a play, he realised. *A Long Day's Journey Into Night* – a microcosm of the Irish will to endure in two or three hours.

'The Irish had not flipped out over "running" it occurs to him, but rather the marathon, the outrageousness of the event that could evoke so much courage and triumph, and so much pain and defeat – all at the same time. They must see a great deal of themselves in it.

'Up ahead, Doheny's Pub throbs with celebrating runners. Ah hell, he figures, ducking inside, there are just some things you just have to drink to.'

An unnamed US-based writer was also wowed by the event. 'Dublin has been compared to the noisier stretches of Boston, as each of the communities along the course vies for honours in cheering and décor. But the Irish sense of humour is the prevailing attitude. In the marathon itself keep an eye out for the T-shirts. Last year's unofficial topper belonged to the weary Irishman whose chest proclaimed "Not tonight, Love!"'

'We had a trickle of overseas runners in the first couple of years but it eventually built up,' recalls Price. Indeed, the 1983 marathon produced its first overseas winner when twenty-four-year-old Belgian Ronny Agten had nearly five minutes to spare from Marty Deane.

Clockwise from below left: Committee member Marion Kavanagh (right) with a French competitor, who was part of the EEC Marathon; Gerry O'Rourke's coach Jimmy Byrne congratulates him on his first win in 1982. Behind them is renowned sports photographer, Ray McManus; 1983 winners Ronny Agten Gerry O'Rourke and Mary Purcell.

In 1988 I was 20 and still in college (NIHE Dublin). I played volleyball and thought I was generally fit. As it was the Dublin millennium I thought I would try and do my first ever marathon in Dublin. I knew nothing about shoes or diet or training plans – I had an old Sony Walkman, which I carried in my hand whilst I went out to train three or four times a week. I remember training to about 17 miles and felt that should be enough to get me through. How wrong I was!!

The big day came. I remember feeling comfortable through the run until about mile nineteen when suddenly I started to feel cramping in my legs. I couldn't understand it as I didn't feel tired. It was just a slow build up of pain in my muscles that steadily got worse. I was hydrating at all the water stations, but it kept getting worse. I finished the run – walking and running the last seven miles – in about 4hrs and 6 minutes. I hadn't arranged for anyone to meet me at the end of the race, so I had to walk to O'Connell Street to get my bus home to Glasnevin! I swore I would never do another marathon.

However, twenty-one years later when the 30th Dublin Marathon came around I decided I would try again; this time I followed a training plan, invested in a pair of runners and was more conscious of my diet. I felt much more prepared. I came in about 4hrs 3mins. Again I was disappointed that the last 6 miles of the race the leg cramping had returned to completely destroy my chance of sub 4 hours.

I continued to run marathons and this cramping in the final six miles continued until 2014 when I entered the Berlin Marathon and learned about salt tablets. I thought I would give them a try and took them for the Berlin marathon; it was a warm day and I was sure my cramping would return. However, to my complete astonishment I had zero cramping through the whole run. I took a salt tablet every 7k and felt great right up to the finish line. I got my PB at a time of 3hrs 54mins. It was quite emotional finishing my eighth marathon attempt and achieving my sub 4 hr goal.

I'll be running the 40th anniversary marathon this year in Dublin – with salt tablets at the ready!

Gavin Quigley, Dublin Marathon 1988 & 2009

Mary Purcell leading the women's race in 1983. A legend of Irish athletics, Purcell emerged on the national scene when she ran 2:04.2 for 800m at Morton Stadium to qualify for the Olympic Games in Munich in 1972. From there Purcell went on to excel across the range of middle-distance events including two Olympic Games and two European Championships. She ran her best marathon time of 2:38.49 in Limerick in 1982.

Mary Purcell won the women's race while Gerry O'Rourke took the wheelchair section for the second time.

The 1984 race was designated the first EEC marathon and the Commission invited the ten member states to send a male and female runner to Dublin for the October race. One of the visitors, Svend-Erik Kristensen from Denmark beat Dick Hooper into second place.

But Hooper's enduring love affair with the race was embellished in the next two years when he became the first runner to win it back to back and remains the only one to secure three wins.

'Everything just clicked in the 1985 race. I felt great and was able to appreciate the whole thing particularly the journey through Raheny. The route went very close to where I live and

Early stages of the 1983
Dublin Marathon. Robert
Shaw (0203), eventual
winner Ronny Agten (0204),
Danny McDaid (wearing
cap), DJ Varley (0021), Peter
Flatman (0208), 1981 winner
Neil Cusack (3), 1982
winner Jerry Kiernan (0001),
and John McLaughlin
(0207).

it was just absolute magic. My only regret was that I didn't go for a faster time, though I did do 2.13.48. But in the bigger scheme of things it didn't matter.

'In 1986 the race was run on a ferociously humid day. I got clear at halfway, but never got that far clear and had a great battle with Marty Deane. I just about got home and as soon as I crossed the line I threw up.'

He was the first to benefit from the introduction of prizes for the winners. He received a car in 1985 and £1,000 the following year. Not surprisingly, generating this prize fund placed additional strain on the organising committee. Nowadays, all the major marathons set aside a sizeable percent of their budget for prize money but back in the mid-eighties this

My Memories of the Marathon

I remember my da, Seanie, a carpenter from Nutgrove in Dublin, taking off for hours on end. It was late 1980s. I was a young teenager with no interest or no idea what he was up to; I was reminded by my ever-patient mam that it involved running miles and miles and miles.

Once, he left Rathfarnham at 6pm for 'a long run'. By 10pm he hadn't arrived home ... 'Leave it until after the *Late Late Show,'* my Mam said ... Still no sign ... Many phone calls later we discovered he was at Stepaside Garda Station, swollen ankle and no chance of making it home on foot.

Secretly, I was delighted he was running, though, as he had been overweight. He loved the personal achievement, as did we. He ran two marathons, best time of 4:10 in 1999. I remember something about socks and timing, but I really had no respect for the enormity of the occasion. I was fourteen, and too into getting home to listen to the top 40 charts!!! Somewhere though, the bug must have bitten.

In 2006, two years after I got married, my da died doing the work he loved; he was laying a floor in a house in Rialto when he had a 'catastrophic' brain haemorrhage. End of life. Less than eight months later in Feb 2007, my son Sean, named after his granda, was born.

Three years later, after my daughter Louise came along, I needed something for myself and started running. Six months months later I was embraced into the open arms of Brothers Pearse AC, and so began one of the best journeys of my life ... many routes, many half marathons, cross country races, and two marathons.

My most poignant moment was during marathon training in 2015, running through Rialto, right by the house where my da passed. I had avoided this road for ten years, but when it's part of a training route and you forget ... we ran by ... I bawled. I will never forget the kindness of my clubmates at that time and since – they are always a great support.

I am no championship runner, but I run from the heart. My best marathon time is 4:14. I am still chasing Seanie's 4:10, as is my brother, it's a family joke. I wish we could have the chats about it with my da, but I know he's on the sidelines... still holding the family record.

Niamh Honer

The winner of the women's race in 1984, Ailish Smith, with results co-ordinator Ned Sweeney.

was a new phenomenon.

Hooper came within touching distance of winning again in 1987, but was thwarted by the combined efforts of the Klimes twins, Pavel and Petr who finished first and second respectively. He was third, just fifteen seconds behind the winner.

Born in Czechoslovakia, the twins had defected to the UK where they were seeking political asylum while earning their living from road races. They had sought appearance fees, but their request was flatly rejected by Alex Sweeney. 'I couldn't understand why we would give appearance money.' He acknowledges that a milk company eventually came up with a cheque for them. 'It had nothing to do with the marathon and I didn't want to know about it.'

By now the drop-off in the number of participants was a serious issue. At first it was scarcely discernible, but when the number of finishers dropped from 7,800 to 4,828 in the space of year in the mid-eighties the alarm bells sounded. The event once described by Con Houlihan as the equivalent of a horizontal Everest was no longer fashionable.

Top left: 1985, Dick Hooper takes the win.

Bottom left: the startline, 1986.

Right: a selection of finshers' plaques made by Copperart.

Ireland's first running boom had run its course. Fewer people were taking up the sport, possibly because the economy had improved and they had less spare time. In order to survive, the marathon would need to attract more overseas runners and a commercial sponsor. The sudden death of long-time commitee-member Ciaran Looney in the spring of 1985 was another serious blow.

Writing in the 1986 official programme, Alex Sweeney – who was the public face of the event – alluded to the race's financial woes.

'I suppose by now most people with just a little interest in running will know of our financial problems. We in Dublin are indeed unique among major marathons around the world in that we depend on the runners' entry fees to finance and support the race. Our numbers are not sufficient to ensure the maintaining of standards and the continued success of this great event.'

The direct intervention of RTE's Director General Vincent Finn essentially saved the 1986 race. He approached Dublin Corporation, Cospóir and Dublin East Regional Tourism and along with RTE they made a grant of £10,500.

Subsequently Dublin Corporation chipped in with an additional £1,500 bringing the total subsidy to £12,000 which made it feasible to run the race.

This was just a stop-gap measure and the event still faced an uncertain future as Frank Greally alluded to in the *Irish Runner* in June 1987. He singled out Radio 2 for particular criticism.

'The enthusiasm of Radio 2 for the event, which the station helped launch eight years ago,

DUBLIN MARATHON 1992

(incorporating the B.L.E. National Marathon Championships
& the N.A.C.A. National Marathon Championship)

(ORGANISED BY THE BUSINESS HOUSES ATHLETIC ASSOCIATION)

Monday, 26th October, 1992
10.00 a.m.

TRAINING GRANTS

MEN		WOMEN	
1st	£1,500	1st	£1,500
2nd	£ 750	2nd	£ 750
3rd	£ 350	3rd	£ 350

WATERFORD CRYSTAL
Waterford Crystal will be awarded
in the mens, womens, wheelchair and cerebral palsy categories.

CLUB CATEGORY
There is a £300 prize fund

WHEELCHAIR CATEGORY
There is a £400 prize fund

CEREBRAL PALSY CATEGORY
There is a £100 prize fund

GENERAL
25 Weekends for 2 to the Yeats Country Hotel,
Westport Woods, or Blooms to be drawn amongst
entrants entered before the closing date.

seems to have flagged in recent times, and although they appear anxious to have their name dominate the event for publicity reasons their commitment to the proper promotion of the race is in doubt.

'It is time that Radio 2 either make a serious commitment to the race or do the honourable thing and move aside to accommodate a major sponsor who could market the race to its full potential,' he wrote.

Similarly in the same edition of the magazine, Dick Hooper suggested that Radio 2 should 'shape up or let go'. Their criticism drew a sharp rebuke from the deputy controller of Radio 2 Louis Hogan, who played a key role in the launch of the marathon.

He pointed out that Radio 2 and the BHAA had recognised for some time that if the marathon was to keep pace with the changing developments in other capital city marathons, a substantial cash boost would be needed probably involving a major sponsor.

'Two years ago, Radio 2 gave the BHAA *carte blanche* to seek such a sponsor, intimating that we would be willing to take a less prominent position should a sponsor be found.'

The event suffered another hammer blow when the Minister for Sport Frank Fahey privately told the organisers that Cospóir's annual grant of £3,000 was been withdrawn in 1987.

The new National Lottery had already grossed £40m in ticket sales in 1987 and the BHAA had hopes that the marathon grant would be doubled. Instead they were left empty-handed. 'It's shameful,' declared Sweeney in an interview with Liam Hayes in the *Sunday Press*. Ultimately the race went ahead as scheduled in 1987. In a curious twist of fate the National Lottery sponsored the marathon in 2011.

Dublin's Millennium celebrations in 1988 – 'Dublin's Great in '88' – gave the marathon an ideal opportunity to promote itself and the public responded with over 9,000 entries – the biggest field for five years. Following promotional work at the London and Paris Marathons and the Great North Run in England, more than a thousand overseas entries were received.

The additional revenue from entry fees boosted finances, though to some extent the race was still run on a wing and prayer. The intervention of supermarket chain Quinnsworth saved the day – they distributed entry forms and supplied t-shirts for the finishers.

But on the eve of the race, RTE dropped a bombshell when they announced that they wouldn't be covering the race live on television as they had done in previous years. In her weekly *Evening Press* running column Lindie Naughton was scathing in her criticism of the decision.

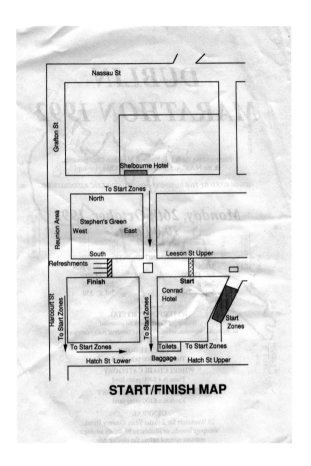

START/FINISH MAP

(Map labels: Nassau St; Grafton St; Shelbourne Hotel; To Start Zones; North; Reunion Area; Stephen's Green; West; East; South; Refreshments; Leeson St Upper; Finish; Harcourt St; To Start Zones; To Start Zones; Start; Conrad Hotel; Start Zones; To Start Zones; Hatch St Lower; Toilets; To Start Zones; Baggage; Hatch St Upper)

PRE-MARATHON EVENTS

Seminar	A Marathon Seminar sponsored by "New Balance" will be held in the Round Room of the Mansion House on Saturday 24th October at 2.00 p.m. Subject: *Pre-Marathon Preparation.* Speaker: *Larry Groellman, University of Pittsburgh Sports Institute.*
Pasta Party	"*ROMA PASTA PARTY*" will be held in the Mansion House on Sunday Night from 8 pm to 11 pm. Entry fee £2.00. *All proceeds will go to the Irish Wheelchair Association.*

YOUR RACE TIMETABLE

Start	Leeson St. Upper (See Map) Arrive no later than 9.00 am Parking will not be allowed near the start/finish area or St. Stephen's Green. Please come dressed to race. There will be no dressing facilities.
9.00—9.15 am	Baggage should be deposited in Lower Hatch St. no later than 9.15 am. Do not leave valuables in the Baggage area. Baggage will be re-located at finish area. Toilets will be located in Hatch St. on your way to the start.
9.15—9.30 am	Start Zones will be located in Lower Hatch St. The Fast Zone will be for the 2.30—3.30 hours runners and the Slow Zone will be for runners over 3.30 hours. No runners will be allowed to the start via Leeson St.
9.50 am 9.55 am 10.00 am	Wheelchair Start Cerebral Palsy Start Marathon Start
Course	(See Map) Be cautious on all roads at all times. Roads will re-open after 5 hours. Clocks will be at the 5-10-15-20 mile marks. Transport and communication will be available at all stations. Medical Stations will be available on route and medical attention is provided by St. Johns Ambulance. (See Map).
Finish	St. Stephen's Green South. (See Map) When you cross the line please keep walking. Do not change chutes as your number will have to be recorded and your computer tag removed for the results.
Plaques	Plaques will be awarded immediately at the end of the chute. Only runners with official numbers intact will receive a plaque. Lost plaques will not be replaced.
Refreshments	Refreshments and baggage will be available after you receive your plaque and cape. EXIT ONLY AT ST. STEPHEN'S GREEN SOUTH/HARCOURT ST.
Re-Union Area	St. Stephens Green Park.
Race Number	Check that you have your correct number. Do not put pins through the computer tag and wear your number on the front. It must not be covered, defaced or interfered with in any way.
Official Finishers	Official recordings of finishers will cease after 4.00 pm. (6 hours).
Results	The provisional results will be available at the Race Night.
Runners Night	All runners are cordially invited to our Race Night in the Garda Club, Harrington Street, starting at 8.00 pm. Admission £2.00.
B.L.E. Championship	Any athletes wishing to enter the B.L.E. Championship must be registered at the B.L.E. desk in the Mansion House.

GOOD LUCK FROM THE BUSINESS HOUSES ATHLETIC ASSOCIATION.

Printed by The Central Remedial Clinic

'So you have the absurd situation where a sporting fixture which is part-sponsored by RTE is to be ignored. The marathon is THE big-city event on October Bank Holiday Monday – the city is closed off almost all day; you can't ignore it. Shame on you RTE.'

Instead of covering the marathon, RTE's outside broadcasting unit headed to Leopardstown to televise the horse racing. 'It's a terrible kick in the arse for us after putting in so much effort,' commented Sweeney. But the marathon went on and Kerryman John Griffin won it in a time of 2:16.02.

The budget for the 1988 millennium marathon was in the region of £125,000. Responding to a letter in the *Irish Times* which queried the race budget, Sweeney gave a full breakdown of the costs.

'The outgoings are extensive and include £50,000 for prizes (cash prizes and plaques for all finishers), £25,000 for heavy equipment like gantry, barriers, portable huts etc, £6,000 for insurance, £8,000 for printing and postage. £2,000 for portable toilets, £2,000 for transport and haulage and £20,000 for office and administration for one year and many other small items of expense.'

RTE finally ended its formal links with the event after the millennium marathon in 1988.

By then Michael Carroll, an enthusiastic supporter of the event had retired. Louis Hogan, meanwhile, moved on to head up Millennium Radio, which RTE established to commemorate the foundation of Dublin in 998.

'I was disappointed that after I moved to Millennium Radio our association with the race was dropped,' said Hogan.

'Noel [Carroll] and I were very proud that Dublin was the first of the European capital cities to stage a people's marathon and even more so of the amount of money it raised for charity down through the years.'

Facing into 1989 the future was bleak unless a title sponsor could be found. Regardless of their financial plight, the BHAA pressed ahead with the race and dipped into their

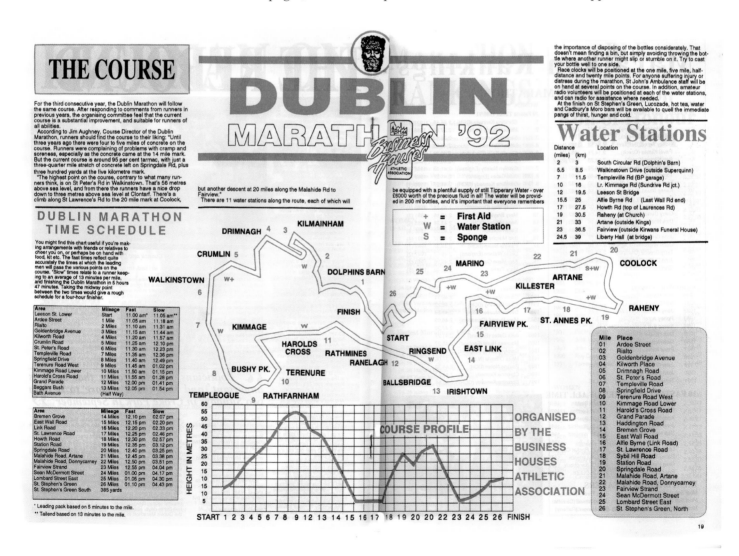

THE COURSE

For the third consecutive year, the Dublin Marathon will follow the same course. After responding to comments from runners in previous years, the organising committee feel that the current course is a substantial improvement, and suitable for runners of all abilities.

According to Jim Aughney, Course Director of the Dublin Marathon, runners should find the course to their liking: "Until three years ago there were four to five miles of concrete on the course. Runners were complaining of problems with cramp and soreness, especially as the concrete came at the 14 mile mark. But the current course is around 95 per cent tarmac, with just a three-quarter mile stretch of concrete left on Springdale Rd, plus three hundred yards at the five kilometre mark.

"The highest point on the course, contrary to what many runners think, is on St Peter's Rd in Walkinstown. That's 56 metres above sea level, and from there the runners have a nice drop down to three metres above sea level at Clontarf. There's a climb along St Lawrence's Rd to the 20 mile mark at Coolock,

but another descent at 20 miles along the Malahide Rd to Fairview."

There are 11 water stations along the route, each of which will

DUBLIN MARATHON TIME SCHEDULE

You might find this chart useful if you're making arrangements with friends or relatives to cheer you on, or perhaps be on hand with food, kit etc. The fast times reflect quite accurately the times at which the leading men will pass the various points on the course. "Slow" times relate to a runner keeping to an average of 13 minutes per mile, and finishing the Dublin Marathon in 5 hours 47 minutes. Taking the midway point between the two times would give a rough schedule for a four-hour finisher.

Area	Mileage	Fast	Slow
Leeson St. Lower	Start	11.00 am*	11.05 am**
Ardee Street	1 Mile	11.05 am	11.18 am
Rialto	2 Miles	11.10 am	11.31 am
Goldenbridge Avenue	3 Miles	11.15 am	11.44 am
Kilworth Road	4 Miles	11.20 am	11.57 am
Crumlin Road	5 Miles	11.25 am	12.10 pm
St. Peter's Road	6 Miles	11.30 am	12.23 pm
Templeville Road	7 Miles	11.35 am	12.36 pm
Springfield Drive	8 Miles	11.40 am	12.49 pm
Terenure Road West	9 Miles	11.45 am	01.02 pm
Kimmage Road Lower	10 Miles	11.50 am	01.15 pm
Harold's Cross Road	11 Miles	11.55 am	01.28 pm
Grand Parade	12 Miles	12.00 pm	01.41 pm
Beggars Bush	13 Miles	12.05 pm	01.54 pm
Bath Avenue	(Half Way)		

Area	Mileage	Fast	Slow
Bremen Grove	14 Miles	12.10 pm	02.07 pm
East Wall Road	15 Miles	12.15 pm	02.20 pm
Link Road	16 Miles	12.20 pm	02.33 pm
St. Lawrence Road	17 Miles	12.25 pm	02.46 pm
Howth Road	18 Miles	12.30 pm	02.57 pm
Station Road	19 Miles	12.35 pm	03.12 pm
Springdale Road	20 Miles	12.40 pm	03.25 pm
Malahide Road, Artane	21 Miles	12.45 pm	03.38 pm
Malahide Road, Donnycarney	22 Miles	12.50 pm	03.51 pm
Fairview Strand	23 Miles	12.55 pm	04.04 pm
Sean McDermott Street	24 Miles	01.00 pm	04.17 pm
Lombard Street East	25 Miles	01.05 pm	04.30 pm
St. Stephen's Green	26 Miles	01.10 pm	04.43 pm
St. Stephen's Green South	385 yards		

* Leading pack based on 5 minutes to the mile.
** Tailend based on 13 minutes to the mile.

DUBLIN MARATHON '92
Business Houses ATHLETIC ASSOCIATION

be equipped with a plentiful supply of still Tipperary Water - over £6000 worth of the precious fluid in all! The water will be provided in 200 ml bottles, and it's important that everyone remembers

+	=	First Aid
W	=	Water Station
S	=	Sponge

the importance of disposing of the bottles considerably. That doesn't mean finding a bin, but simply avoiding throwing the bottle where another runner might slip or stumble on it. Try to cast your bottle well to one side.

Race clocks will be positioned at the one mile, five mile, half-distance and twenty mile points. For anyone suffering injury or distress during the marathon, St John's Ambulance staff will be on hand at several points on the course. In addition, amateur radio volunteers will be positioned at each of the water stations, and can radio for assistance where needed.

At the finish on St Stephen's Green, Lucozade, hot tea, water and Cadbury's Moro bars will be available to quell the immediate pangs of thirst, hunger and cold.

Water Stations

Distance (miles)	(km)	Location
2	3	South Circular Rd (Dolphin's Barn)
5.5	8.5	Walkinstown Drive (outside Superquinn)
7	11.5	Templeville Rd (BP garage)
10	16	Lr. Kimmage Rd (Sundrive Rd jct.)
12	19.5	Leeson St Bridge
15.5	25	Alfie Byrne Rd (Last Wall Rd end)
17	27.5	Howth Rd (top of Laurences Rd)
19	30.5	Raheny (at Church)
21	33	Artane (outside Kings)
23	36.5	Fairview (outside Kirwans Funeral House)
24.5	39	Liberty Hall (at bridge)

ORGANISED BY THE BUSINESS HOUSES ATHLETIC ASSOCIATION

COURSE PROFILE

Mile	Place
01	Ardee Street
02	Rialto
03	Goldenbridge Avenue
04	Kilworth Place
05	Drimnagh Road
06	St. Peter's Road
07	Templeville Road
08	Springfield Drive
09	Terenure Road West
10	Kimmage Road Lower
11	Harold's Cross Road
12	Grand Parade
13	Haddington Road
14	Bremen Grove
15	East Wall Road
16	Alfie Byrne (Link Road)
17	St. Lawrence Road
18	Sybil Hill Road
19	Station Road
20	Springdale Road
21	Malahide Road, Artane
22	Malahide Road, Donnycarney
23	Fairview Strand
24	Sean McDermott Street
25	Lombard Street East
26	St. Stephen's Green, North

reserve fund to the tune of £16,000. Furthermore, the prize fund was slashed from £26,000 to £5,000. Worse still, there was a two-third drop in the number of entries compared to the millennium marathon.

Help came from an unlikely source. Following a series of winters during which Dublin city was engulfed in thick black smog, the government announced that a ban on the sale, marketing, and distribution of 'smoky' coal would be introduced.

CDL Coalite, a company which had to restructure their business model due to the new regulations, agreed to sponsor the race in a three-year deal. As their slogan said: 'CDL Coalite are happy to keep the Dublin City Marathon flame burning'. The race was re-branded the CDL Coalite Dublin Marathon.

The company poured £50,000 into the 1989 race most of which, ironically, was used to fund RTE TV's live coverage of it. However, no cash prizes were paid to the winners due to

Left: Some spiritual
guidance as the runners
near Fairview.

Below: Light the Flame:
CDL Coalite were the
first title sponsors of
the Dublin Marathon
in 1989. Pictured
at the sponsorship
announcement are
Alex Sweeney, Marion
Kavanagh, Eugene
Gibney, managing
director CDL, and Billy
Kennedy.

a surprise intervention by BLE.

They informed the organisers that cash prizes were banned because they would infringe the athletes' amateur status. Instead any cash prizes had to be paid into a trust fund. The BHAA were anxious not to get involved in another confrontation with BLE and reluctantly went along with the directive.

Indeed, the improved relationship between the two organisations was emphasised in 1991 when the event was designated as the BLE National Marathon and the trial race for the 1992 Barcelona Olympics. Jerry Kiernan made a triumphant return winning his second Dublin Marathon while three-time winner Dick Hooper was fourth.

Chapter 8

Death of a Hero

Left: Noel Carroll,
7 December 1941 –
23 October 1998.

Behind the scenes there was a changing of the guard in the Dublin Marathon in the 1990s. Throughout the decade it was a perennial struggle to keep the race alive. In 1998 the organisers also had to deal with the incalculable loss of its founder Noel Carroll, who died prematurely on the eve of the race. By then, however, the initiatives which ultimately not alone saved the race, but established it again as one of the country's premier sporting events, were being formulated.

But in the early 1990s the Dublin Marathon went perilously close to the edge. The financial crisis began as the CDL sponsorship deal was not renewed when its initial three-year term expired in 1991.

RTE dispatched reporter Ken Murray to cover the 1992 marathon – which had no title sponsor – for TV news. He anticipated filing a run of the mill race report. Instead, he stumbled upon a scoop: the marathon was in grave danger of going out of business.

'Basically I was told that unless the organisers found a sponsor within six weeks they

would lose their date on the international marathon calendar, which would effectively be the end of the race. I did my report along the lines that there was just six weeks left to save the Dublin Marathon.'

Months later he discovered his report had played a significant role in saving the event. After seeing it on the TV news, Neville Galloway, marketing director of the Golden Pages suggested to the company's then managing director Mike Murphy and its public relations director Margaret McKeon-Boyle that they begin talks with the BHAA with a view to saving the race.

The upshot was that the marathon's future was secured for the next three years through a sponsorship deal with the company. An added bonus was that the marathon entry form was published in the Golden Pages, which had a print run of 450,000 and was distributed nationwide.

According to Alex Sweeney the deal came at a price. 'While they were a great sponsor they killed me with the workload. They wanted value for money and they bloody got it.' Sweeney took early retirement in 1993 when he was fifty-two and spent the next few years working as a full-time volunteer with the BHAA and the marathon.

Left: Frank Greally, second from right, pictured at the Gratitude Run in Morton Stadium on 18 August 2015 to mark the 45th anniversary of his junior record for 10,000m. Also pictured are Catherina McKiernan (left) and Jim McNamara (right).

Below: Haile Gebrselassie, Jim Aughney and Catherina McKiernan at a photocall in London. Gebrselassie has won two Olympic gold medals and four World Championship titles in the 10,000 metres. He also won the Berlin Marathon four times consecutively and the Dubai Marathon three times consecutively.

Perhaps his biggest legacy to the marathon was his recruitment of Jim Aughney. Raised on a farm in Roscat near Tullow, County Carlow, Aughney's first memory of the Dublin Marathon was listening to John Saunders' live radio commentary in 1980. Career options were limited for school leavers in the late 1970s. 'In those days, career guidance consisted of being handed an application form for the Gardaí, the ESB and the Department of Posts and Telegraphs. Going to University didn't enter into it.'

He joined the Department of Posts and Telegraphs as a trainee technician. He spent some time in Dublin, but was primarily based in Waterford for the next three years. In those days the Department had a unique way of deciding where to post their technicians once their training was completed. Those who fared best in the final exams were sent to Dublin while the remainder were posted to the rest of Ireland. Aughney ended up in Dublin.

Having started running while living in Waterford, he was pleasantly surprised to discover there was a thriving inter-firms running scene in the capital. Better still, the Department of P & T – later re-branded Telecom Eireann – had a crack team.

'It got to the stage where it was embarrassing because we were winning all the races. I pointed out to the others on the team that we were winning everything, but not putting on any race ourselves. Everybody thought the race was a great idea and asked me when I was organising it.'

He assembled a team and organised a road race in Kimmage Manor on Dublin's southside. After the prizes were presented Sweeney approached Aughney and told him he wanted him for a job! The Carlow man had no idea what he was letting himself in for.

Throughout the next decade Aughney filled a variety of roles on the marathon committee. 'The committee meetings were legendary. A lot of them took place on a Saturday and could last all day. Financially it was a real struggle and the budget meetings used to be very interesting.'

A natural leader, Aughney also rose through the ranks of the BHAA and was chairman when Sweeney intimated in 1996 that he wanted to step down as marathon director. 'Basically he said 'Here's the ball.' So we had to run with it.'

The day-to-day humdrum of organising the marathon paled into the shadows when news broke on the afternoon of Friday, 23 October 1998 – three days before the race – that Noel Carroll had died suddenly after suffering a heart attack while out on his daily lunchtime run around UCD.

Frank Greally, his lifelong friend and confidant was driving past Christ Church Cathedral in Dublin's city centre later that afternoon when his mobile phone rang. He took the call from his work colleague Conor O'Hagan who told him the sad news.

'All I remember is going blank,' recalls Greally. 'I don't know how long I sat there in the car before I became aware that a taxi-driver was beeping continuously at me and pointing back the road. I looked in the mirror and there was a line of traffic behind as far as I could see.'

Carroll and Greally met regularly for lunch in Dublin City Hall. 'He would be coming back after a run in College Park and would unwrap his sandwiches and he always had a spare one for me. We'd talk about music, literature and running and at weekends we often went walking up Djouce Mountain.'

Jim Aughney remembers being in the Gresham Hotel that same Friday, meeting and greeting American runners who were taking part in the marathon, when he received a phone call from Greally to tell him the news. 'Everybody was speechless.'

While Carroll was the public face of the marathon when the organisers were at loggerheads with BLE, his work behind the scenes often went unheralded. 'Noel was brilliant,' recalls Billy Kennedy, who was the marathon's operations director for thirteen years. 'I would often ring him up looking for something to be done and he'd always say "Leave it with me, Billy". Whatever I asked always got done.'

He was mostly unflappable, though occasionally he lost his cool. Former race administrator Marion Kavanagh recalls accompanying him in the lead car for the marathon in the era before road closures and when there was a perennial shortage of stewards.

'Basically the lead car would have to clear the route. One time we were travelling through Finglas and there was such a huge crowd out that the leaders got ahead of the race car. It was a potentially disastrous situation and it was the one time he wasn't sure of what to do next.' The crisis was averted when they got past the leading runners shortly afterwards.

There was poignancy about his death as he had written about the well-being of athletes' hearts in *The Runner's Book*.

'Don't talk too much about hearts either. I was on the *Late Late Show* the night the camera man passed out when Arthur Ashe mentioned his heart condition. Hearts bother people. And talking about your heart to a loved one creates all sorts of fears about heart attacks and related fatal blows. A runner can take it for granted that his immediate family does worry about him. I know it should be the other way around, but it's not.

'No matter, how absolute the available evidence on the safety of running is, there will always be doubt. In reality a person going out for a night on the town is taking a far greater risk than a runner going for a few miles trot. But you may have a job on your hands trying to convince your loved ones that it's true.'

A year before his death his four children, Enda, Nicola, Noel and Stephen ran in the New York Marathon to raise funds for GOAL, the third world charity which he chaired. 'He spoke to each of us individually afterwards on the phone and listened to our different experiences,' recalls Enda. On the tenth anniversary of his death in 2008, they ran the Dublin Marathon as a family in his memory.

From a very early age, his children were aware that his job as public relations officer of Dublin Corporation meant he was in the public eye. They were taught to be quiet when he was on the phone because the odds were he could be doing a live radio interview,' recalls Enda.

His daughters were in their teens when he became involved in organising the first Dublin Marathon. 'I remember hearing his advice slots on the radio. Before the race, there was a bit of anxiousness around the house because of his participation. He wasn't a marathon runner. He said afterwards that the marathon "wall" was real and he had hit it on Nutley Lane,' said Enda.

'He ran 3.09 in his first marathon, which was his best time and one which he was really proud off. He probably should have done just the one because he was so busy. He had a full-time job, four children, was writing articles for newspapers, involved in organising the event and he had to find time to do his own training,' says Nicola.

Athletics was his passion according to his daughters. 'He used to say his job was his hobby and his hobby was his job,' recalls Nicola. Running almost certainly prolonged his life as his autopsy revealed that he had a heart condition, possibly from birth, but being so fit helped camouflage it.

Nonetheless, he probably suffered a number of minor heart attacks over the years. Unfortunately they were never detected as he had an aversion to attending doctors. 'It was devastating for us to learn this because he could still be with us today had the condition been detected,' said Enda.

Before the start of the 1998 marathon in O'Connell Street, Greally paid a moving tribute to the man without whom there would almost certainly never have been a marathon through the streets of Dublin city centre. The runners, officials and spectators observed a minute's silence in his memory.

Nowadays, he is commemorated annually with the race winner being presented with the Noel Carroll trophy.

Noel Carroll's daughter,
Enda Carroll, presents the
Noel Carroll trophy to 2018
Dublin Marathon winner,
Asefe Bekele.

The Phoenix Rises

JIM Aughney had very definite ideas about what he wanted to achieve when he took over as director of the Dublin Marathon in 1997.

He disbanded the existing race committee, replaced it with a smaller group of his running colleagues from Telecom Eircom, club mates from Civil Service AC and some survivors from the old committee. The process of establishing the marathon as a stand-alone event was set in motion. There were fewer BHAA officials on the new committee and the marathon was dropped from the association's schedule of races. From then, the two organisations forged separate identities and gradually grew apart. Their fortunes sharply diverged as well. Now, the marathon is prospering while the BHAA is struggling to recapture the halcyon days of the past.

He brought a new level of professionalism to the organisation of the marathon. Less was left to chance. Up until then they depended on the goodwill of the Gardaí to supply safety barriers free of charge – they rarely had enough. In the new regime the number of barriers needed was calculated and hired from an outside supplier. So they never ran short again. This was symptomatic of the changes introduced.

Attention to detail is what separates good events from great events. Jim, supported by the new committee – all of whom were experienced marathoners – had the vision, drive and commitment to prepare the event for the challenges ahead in the new millennium.

However, before a single reform could be initiated they had to secure a new sponsor. The Golden Pages' deal – which was extended for another year – came to an end after the 1996 race. The committee

THE DUBLIN MARATHON

successfully pitched to Dublin-based radio station 98FM, who came on board as the new title sponsors. Gear manufacturers Adidas later joined them as associate sponsors.

For the first time in the history of the race finishers were presented with a medal instead of a plaque after the 1997 race. The plaques were back the following year, but were permanently replaced by medals in 2003. Back in 1997 the organisers had bigger issues to deal with.

For the marathon to survive it had to increase the number of participants. The committee toyed with the idea of introducing a relay event in which team members each run a specific distance, an innovation which was successfully introduced in the Belfast Marathon.

'We knew it was a good source of revenue, but we decided to focus all our attention on trying to get more people to run the race. In the event of our efforts failing we could look at the relay option again, whereas if we introduced it straight away there was no going back,' said Aughney.

I run regularly these days, but a decade ago I was not that into exercise. So I'm not sure why my New Year's Resolution for 2007 was to take part in the Dublin Marathon. Not run it, but walk it. I mentioned this to my family and before the application deadline was up, I had two companions – my younger sister, Laura, and my Dad, Sean.

Everyone talks about the great atmosphere and the friendliness of the Dublin Marathon and we certainly experienced that. Family, friends and neighbours all popped up at various points along the course. One of my favourite moments was when we passed Dick Hooper marshalling in Ballsbridge – an athlete we had cheered for in the past as he zoomed along the top of our road on his home turf of Raheny, but this time it was us competing and him cheering.

It was shortly after that point that we abandoned Dad. Grand Canal, Mile 24, I think. The three of us just wanted it over at that point. Dad was visibly in pain, and I suspect we were driving him mad asking him if he was all right. (At least, that's what I tell myself to ease the guilt of leaving him behind.) I quietly decided in those two miles that I might have enough in the tank to leave Laura behind at the last minute too. (Anyone who knows us will testify that we're a competitive family). As we turned into Merrion Square, I looked at her and said the words 'sprint finish'. I now realise that was really silly – being six years younger than me she was considerably fitter than me and pipped me to the post. I should have said nothing! Dad crossed the line less than two minutes later. It had taken us just over six hours. We were delighted with ourselves.

Looking back at the results now, I remember Laura and I were not impressed at all to be listed as from 'Gbr' rather than 'Irl' - even if it was technically correct as we both live in London and had travelled home for the marathon. It must have been quite the sticking point as we both managed to get ourselves listed as Irish athletes for our return to the Dublin Marathon the following year!

Mile 24, 2008: we abandoned Dad again. But turning into Merrion Square the second year, I was taking no chances. I am very proud to have been the first of the Powers to cross the line in the last marathon we did together. And we all took 25 minutes off our previous time. We've talked about doing it again, but the timing hasn't been right since. I suspect none of us have ruled it out completely, but it probably wouldn't be right without the other two!

Lisa Power

The marathon had a lucky break when London Marathon director Dave Bedford rejected an approach from North American-based charities seeking to secure places in London. Aughney reasoned that if American based runners were willing to cross the Atlantic to compete in London, they might be persuaded to come to Dublin instead.

The new sponsors 98FM were receptive to the idea of attracting overseas runners. Part of their marketing budget was spent on promoting the event at the expos of major international marathons. During a trip to the New York Marathon's expo Liam O'Riain, a key figure on the new committee, met representatives from a number of the charities and invited them to send runners to the 1998 Dublin Marathon.

Three hundred and fifty-six came that first year. They were treated royally to ensure their trip was memorable for all the right reasons. A special desk was set up in the Gresham Hotel where they could collect their race number. Dublin lived up to its sobriquet of being the 'Friendly Marathon'.

Over the next four years, runners and their support teams from US and Canadian-based charities, Joints in Motion, Team Diabetes and Team in Training flocked to Dublin. Essentially they saved the marathon. At the turn of the millennium there were more runners from the US and Canada running in Dublin than Irish runners. At its peak there were five

Above left: Runners make their way through the Phoenix Park..

Above right: 2009 winners Kateryna Stetsenko (Ukraine) 2:32.45 and Feyisa Lilesa (Ethiopia) 2:09.12.

Right: The pain and the pride.

thousand participants from overseas charities as the number of finishers grew from 3,123 in 1997 to 7,156 in 2000.

The devastating 9/11 attacks in the US reverberated globally. There were grim warnings that air travel would never recover. But marathoners are a different breed. The majority of the American-based runners turned up as scheduled to run in the 2001 Dublin Marathon less than seven weeks after the two passenger jets had been deliberately flown into the World Trade Centre in New York.

Nonetheless, Aughney reasoned that it was virtually inevitable there would be a drop-off in American participants in future years. 'So we started looking around for new ideas.' Frank Greally and Paul Moloney, a sales executive with Adidas – who took over as the title sponsors of the marathon in 2001 – and Aughney travelled to London in early 2002 to attend a seminar about the business relationship between UK charities and the London Marathon.

'The return flight was delayed and the three of us were sitting around in the airport. Basi-

An aerial view of the start, 1993.

119

cally we were just hopping balls,' recalls Aughney, who half in jest suggested to Greally that with the *Irish Runner*'s twentieth anniversary coming up 'it was about time he did something for Irish athletics'. Paul Moloney chipped in with the idea of organising a road race promising that Adidas would sponsor it.

By the time their flight was called the idea had grown into a race series – comprising a five mile, a ten mile and a half marathon to be sponsored by Adidas. 'A lot of things like that are just banter and there is no follow through,' admitted Greally.

But Aughney and Moloney were driven individuals while Greally felt he owed Adidas a favour. In its early years, the survival of *Irish Runner* magazine owed much to the generosity of Michael O'Connell, the managing director of Three Stripe International, Adidas's Irish licensee, who funded a double-page colour advertisement in every issue.

As soon as the trio returned to their desks the project was set in motion. At the time Dublin Bus organised a ten-mile race under the auspices of the BHAA. Unfortunately, they weren't interested in their event being part of a new race series. Aughney then approached Civil Service AC who hosted the annual Frank Duffy ten-mile race, a prestigious event which attracted mostly elite runners. It was launched by Civil Service AC to commemorate Frank Duffy, who coached Noel Carroll for the 1968 Olympics, after they turned down his suggestion to organise a marathon.

'I sat down with Civil Service and I guaranteed them that they wouldn't suffer any losses if they came on board, though my promise to get them a thousand entries was treated with some incredulity,' recalled Aughney. Greally organised a new five-mile race in the Phoenix Park, while the BHAA, who already ran a half marathon in the Phoenix Park every September, agreed that the race would become part of the series.

The Adidas Marathon Race Series was launched in 2002. There was no guarantee it would be a success. Indeed, the Dublin Marathon committee set up a separate company to oversee the project. It was a precautionary measure – in the event of it sinking they didn't want the marathon to be burdened with the financial losses.

The exact opposite happened. This was the single most influential factor in deciding the fate of the Dublin Marathon. Not alone was the race series a runaway success, it proved the ideal recruiting ground for new marathoners.

Having coped with five, ten and 13.1-mile races, the next logical step for runners was to tackle the marathon. The timing of the race series during the late summer was ideally suited as they could be incorporated into a training schedule for the Dublin Marathon.

But it is no coincidence either that Ireland's second running boom happened at the same time as the country was experiencing another economic tsunami. Unemployment had rocketed and people had more free time.

From 2002 onwards the numbers participating in the marathon grew consistently until in 2008, 9,316 runners – the highest number ever – finished the race. A year later another milestone was reached when the Dublin Marathon had its highest entry ever, surpassing the 1983 record of 11,264 and a new record (10,413) of finishers.

This was a personal landmark for Aughney because when he took over as race director

Below left: the Garda Athletics Club on the startline.

Below right: a general view of the field, 2012.

his initial target was to bring the number of participants back up to the 1983 level. The rest of the committee were sceptical. 'They used to laugh their head off whenever I mentioned it.' His other target of seeing Jerry Kiernan's long established fastest time of 2:13.45 being broken was achieved in 2004 when Kenyan Lezan Kimutai ran 2:13.07.

By now, the Dublin Marathon had a new headquarters. Having been tenants in various locations in the city centre, they found a permanent home in the Donore Harriers' AC clubhouse in Chapelizod adjacent to the Phoenix Park. Initially, they had to make do with a windowless office, but the advantage of the site was that it had storage facilities. They later moved to a bigger space in the clubhouse.

In the early 1980s the race's HQ was in the basement of 24 Upper Fitzwilliam Street in Dublin city centre. Kevin Sweeney, then a student in Trinity College, worked there during the summer months. 'Every morning I'd get a taxi to Sheriff Street Post Office to collect the postbag with the race entries.'

Each entry was manually allocated a race number, while all entry fees had to be collated and counted. 'In the afternoon we would lodge the money in the Baggot Street branch of Bank of Ireland where Dominic Branigan, a member of the organising committee, worked.'

Nowadays, runners can enter most races with the click of a mouse. Few had heard of on-line entries when Aughney first mooted the idea. Every entry was done on paper. It was time-consuming to input the entries and errors occurred because names and addresses were misread. 'I felt there must be a better way of doing it, but when I went to companies with the idea of an on-line system they laughed at me.'

He persisted and eventually found a US company Active.com who had pioneered an on-line entry system for college registration. Better still, they had developed a system to be used for races which needed to be tested. So over the next couple of months, the gremlins were found and corrected. Now the Dublin Marathon had an innovative on-line system. Within two years, the number of paper entries dropped from 100 per cent to five percent.

The Dublin Marathon was also at the forefront of the technological revolution which transformed how road races are timed and results compiled. In the formative years, an army of volunteers were deployed to record the race number of each individual, which required the complicated use of a multi-chute system.

In the early spring of 2017 we were all proverbial 'couch potatoes', sitting uncomfortably on the wrong side of the half century. Many good intentions to stay fit had regrettably passed us by and age now seemed an acceptable excuse to limit exercise to a casual walk with the dog or a stroll in the local park when time allowed. One of those casual walks with my little dog along the Ulster Canal Greenway in Monaghan Town in April 2017 led to a chance encounter and an extended conversation with Monaghan's very own marathon man, Leslie Crawford, who was by then in training to complete his 200th marathon. Ever humble about his amazing running record, Leslie remarked that anyone could run a marathon if they put their mind to it and were prepared to commit the required time and energy to a proper training regime. Before we parted that evening Leslie threw down a gauntlet and I sheepishly accepted.

By the following Saturday morning nine raw recruits gathered at an appointed time and place to begin a fledgling over-50s walk-to-jog group that in time would grow into a significant local health and fitness phenomenon known as the Monaghan Town Over-50s Joggernutts. Slowly but surely, with Leslie's guidance and support, confidence and fitness levels increased to the extent that 5km and 10km fun runs became realistic targets that were eventually surpassed. In the summer of 2017 as increasing numbers joined the group a new colourful t-shirt was unveiled to give the Joggernutts a visible identity and a feeling of community.

As the winter of 2017 approached, eight brave hopefuls began preparations for the 2018 Dublin Marathon. The dedication devoted to the training programme was matched by copious social engagements where endless cups of tea and coffee were consumed, experiences shared, injuries diagnosed and treatments considered and most importantly, friendships solidified. Battling through the wind, sleet and hail showers of January and February 2018 made us wonder at our own sanity and at Leslie's better judgement, but on we went in the knowledge that there was a distant goal and hopefully brighter days to come.

To step out on the starting line that crisp and autumn morning in October 2018 with those who had known both your pain and commitment was in itself an enriching experience. What the training had not prepared us for was the amazing carnival atmosphere all along the 26.2-mile route that brought us through the beautiful Phoenix Park and the historic and winding streets of Dublin City. To see first-hand the organisational detail and commitment demonstrated by so many volunteers along the route made us immensely proud of our capital city's capacity to hold such a high-profile event.

We all crossed the finishing line in various states, cheered on by the busload of family and friends who had excitedly travelled with us from Monaghan earlier that morning. We had pushed ourselves far beyond our wildest expectations and in the process shared a memorable experience that will forever bind us together in friendship. When Leslie Crawford threw down that gauntlet, little did he know that he had kindled the flame of a life changing experience that will endure in our memories for the rest of our days.

Enda Galligan, Dublin Marathon 2018

There were incremental improvements in the first half of the eighties with the timing being done automatically, though it still required a significant level of expertise and a large number of volunteers to operate the system. 'It wasn't sustainable particularly if we wanted to grow the numbers in the marathon.'

During their trips abroad to international marathons, committee members were able to keep abreast with the rapid advances being made using chip timing. Initially the new timing chip had to be attached to the runner's shoes. Then a Japanese company developed a J-chip which was incorporated into the runner's number.

In 2004, an Italian company TDS developed a timing system using a tiny electronic device embedded in the runner's race number. It was reliable, disposable and relatively cheap. A team from TDS, based in the small Italian town of Spinea, travelled to Dublin to operate the system and generate the results for the marathon and the race series. Eventually, other timing companies were able to offer a similar service and a Welsh company TDL is now responsible for the timing and results in the marathon and race series.

Efforts have been ongoing over the years to make the event more spectator-friendly.

Clockwise: Esther Macharia wins the women's race in 2014; Patrick Monahan, winner of the wheelchair race; Esther Macharia and Eliud Tao at the prizegiving, 2014, the Gardaí walk to the start, A helping hand; the 2014 medal, commemorating the Battle of Clontarf in 1014.

SSE Airtricity DUBLIN MARATHON 2014

Dublin Marathon 2014

Dublin Marathon 2014

PROUD FINISHER

Dublin Marathon 2014

Dublin Marathon 2014

After the early years, the number of spectators dwindled alarmingly and for a time the support crews and friends of the American charity runners outnumbered the local support along most of the route.

As course director of the race, Aughney suggested to the statutory authorities that a specific route for the race should be agreed on a long-term basis rather that the traditional policy of constant change. The organisers were also looking for a faster course, which ultimately resulted in the race being rerouted away from much of the north-east of the city.

Having a set course was helpful to spectators as they became accustomed to going to a specific spot to watch the race. Entertainment zones were created and expanded for children when Spar was an associate sponsor of the race. The concept was based on the premise that if there was a safe environment for kids to play adjacent to the route, their parents would stay out and watch the race.

On occasions a spot of lateral thinking was deployed to entice more people out on the course. Prior to the Luas works, the route passed very close to the finish in Merrion Square, but then veered right past Pearse Street Dart station and around the perimeter of Trinity College with the runners approaching the finish via Nassau Street.

'I felt anybody walking down Grafton Street wouldn't bother going to Merrion Square to see the race, but they might be enticed to watch from Nassau Street and for years we had a terrific atmosphere in that street with big crowds,' said Aughney.

Above left: Proud finishers Aideen O'Connor, Sinead Hartnett and Thomas Frayne, Clonliffe Harriers AC, 2018.

Above right: Volunteers distributing medals, 2018.

Right: Nearing the finish line in 2013.

The last big frontier for the marathon was bringing it forward by twenty-four hours and staging it on a Sunday. While the original Bank Holiday Monday had served the event well, it became increasingly obvious that having the race on a Sunday would not just make the event more attractive to overseas runners, but also to the Irish market.

The twin influences of the Catholic Church and the Garda Síochána ruled out any change for years. Normally only a skeleton Garda staff is on duty on a Sunday. Furthermore, morning mass attendees might be discommoded if the race occurred on the Sabbath day. 'It's fair to say that we didn't want to take on the Gardaí and the Church together,' says Aughney.

Even though Sunday morning mass attendances dropped over the years, the matter was left sit. Occasionally, when it was raised the relevant bodies ruled it out.

In the end Dublin Tourism did the heavy lifting and persuaded the various civil bodies to accept the change. Aughney allowed himself a wry smile when he received a call from

Dublin Marathon 2013

Above: Members of the Polish Runners Club Ireland, a social running group for the Polish community in Ireland.

a Dublin City Council official to ascertain whether he would be interested in moving the race to a Sunday. 'I said I'd have to discuss it at the next committee meeting, but we had one scheduled for the following night.'

The first 'Sunday' Dublin Marathon was held in 2016 which coincided with the centenary celebrations for the 1916 rising. There were two schools of thought about the unprecedented surge in entries from 15,000 in 2015 to a sell-out record of 19,500 in 2016. One view was the increase was due to the 1916 commemorations – a special medal had been minted for all the finishers. Others speculated that the change in day was mainly responsible for the thirty percent increase in entries.

'There was no way of knowing for sure until we saw the entries for the 2017 race,' said Aughney. The capacity was increased to 20,000 and the race sold out; the pattern was repeated in 2019 and this year's race was sold out in forty days. 'Never in my wildest dream did I ever imagine that would happen.'

An extra 2,500 places were made available in July and a refund system was launched for those who had already entered, but who no longer wanted to run. These extra places sold out the morning they were released, with over eight thousand people applying for the 2,500 places, meaning 2019 will have a record of 22,500 entries. The upper limit was fixed at that number, 'I've no doubt we could sell 25,000 entries, maybe more, but that would start to impact on quality. So we have to control the numbers.'

Ireland is the twenty-ninth-most-populated country in Europe yet the sell-out 2019 Dublin Marathon, which will be sponsored by KBC Bank this year will be the fourth-largest city marathon in Europe. The phoenix has truly risen.

Dublin Marathon 2014

Chapter 10

New Broom Sweeps Clean

But though the numbers taking part in the event continued to grow in the second decade of the new millennium, the standard at elite level in Irish marathon running had fallen dramatically. John Treacy ended his marathon career on a winning note in the 1993 Dublin Marathon crossing the line in 2:14.20. The Los Angeles Olympic silver medallist was the last Irishman to win the race until Sean Hehir's triumph in 2013, the year no overseas elite runners were invited due primarily to the lack of a title sponsor.

Granted, the level of competition at elite level increased in the wake of William Musyoki becoming the first African athlete to win the race in 1995. Unfortunately at the same time, the standard of Irish marathon running sank to a pitiful low.

The ever-consistent John Griffin – who was a back-to-back winner in 1988 and 1989 –

comfortably broke 2:20 when he finished third in 1994. But eighteen years passed before the next Irish-born marathoner, Belfast doctor Paul Pollock, dipped under 2:20 in Dublin, when he finished ninth in 2:16.30.

Tommy Maher (1997), Noel Cullen (1999), Gary Crossan (2003) and Michael O'Connor (2008) all missed the 2:20 mark by less than a minute, while Moldovan-born Sergiu Ciobanu – who later became an Irish citizen and represented the country in international championships – ran 2:19.33 to finish twelfth in 2010.

In the last quarter of a century Ireland has produced three world-class distance runners: Catherina McKiernan, Sonia O'Sullivan and Sinead Diver. Catherina McKiernan, who won the Berlin, London and Amsterdam Marathons and holds the Irish record of 2:22.23, never raced in Dublin. Sinead Diver from Belmullet, who finished seventh in the 2019 London Marathon in 2:24.11 at the age of forty-two, now lives in Australia and represents her adopted country in championship races.

The Dublin Marathon holds so many fond (and not so fond!) memories for me. I've completed it a number of times, but it's the third trip around the course that will be forever ingrained in my memory – trying and failing to go sub-3. Training had gone well and I was confident going into the race. Nicely paced run around the first half of the course and I went through the halfway point on 1:28. Was motoring for much of the second half, but on the dreaded hills around Clonskeagh it started to feel like running in treacle. Head down and pushed on. Coming down Westmoreland Street I was confident that I had done enough, but a glance at the watch with 500 metres to go made me realise it was tighter than I thought. Went hell for leather and crossed the line with 3:00.24 on the finish line clock. I hadn't stopped my watch, but surely it took me more than 24 seconds to cross the start line and my chip time would put me on the right side of 3 hours?

Twenty minutes later I received two texts. One from a non-running friend congratulating me, and another from a running friend commiserating with me. The chip time had just appeared on the website – 3:00.00! I had missed the goal by a fraction of a second. All that I needed to have done was to take one corner a bit tighter or not deviated from my running line to cross the road to family and friends. But what an achievement – you couldn't run such a precise time if you tried!

The sub-3 eventually came in other marathons, but the 3:00.00 story is the one I've told more than any other.

Kieran O'Leary

Above left: Sergiu Ciobanu is crowned National Champion in 2016.

Above right: Gary Crossan, partner of Maria McCambridge, pushes their son, Dylan, in the 2012 marathon.

Sonia O'Sullivan is the only one of the three to have run the Dublin Marathon, which she won on her debut in 2000, just five weeks after securing an Olympic silver medal in the 5,000m at the Sydney Olympics.

O'Sullivan's unexpected appearance at the start of the 2000 race caused some surprise to the elite female runners who were eyeing up the first prize of €8,000 and hadn't counted on her presence. In truth, O'Sullivan was a bit surprised to be warming up for her first marathon.

'It wasn't something that was on my radar. But three weeks before the race I met the British marathon runner Richard Nerurkar in a café in London. He mentioned he was going to Dublin for the marathon and when I checked the date I discovered I would be in Dublin on that day for the launch of my book. I remember saying "Maybe I'll run the marathon".

'Athletics-wise, I was looking for something to do. After the Olympics I had done the usual award ceremonies and presentations. I wanted to get myself focused on running again. I contacted my coach Alan Storey and he said I could do it as a long run. Up until then I had never run longer than two hours. I decided I better do a couple of long runs, which I did on the next two Sundays. I rang Jim Aughney and asked was there any chance of getting a race number and he assured me he would have one for me on the morning of the race.'

But her plan hit another obstacle on the eve of the race. She was due to fly from Cork Airport to Dublin, but the plane slid off the runway. 'We were given vouchers to get some-

thing to eat, but there wasn't a lot of choice. In the end a replacement plane was found and we made it to Dublin late on Sunday night.'

Her memory of the race is dominated by the weather as the runners had to contend with heavy rain and strong winds. 'I wore a t-shirt underneath my singlet and I never took it off because it was so cold. I was never so happy to see the finishing line in my life. I got very tired over the last five or six miles, but I kept thinking it's easier to keep going to the finish than drop out.'

She was twentieth overall and first women in 2:35.42. 'I have never been so sore after a race. The next day we were flying to New York for a holiday. I never felt so much pain as I did walking up the steps to the plane.'

Maria McCambridge is the only Irish female winner since O'Sullivan in 2000.

Dick Hooper, who dipped under the 2:20 barrier on twenty-one occasions, believes the Celtic Tiger contributed to the fall-off in the numbers running the marathon which fed into the drop in standards at elite level.

'Everyone was so distracted making money and having a good time. People weren't prepared

Dublin Marathon 2012

My da started running before I was born. He ran the Dublin Marathon back in its early years and he ran all the classic old races like the Rathcoole 10 and the Dublin Bus 10. Marathon Monday we'd always go in to support him and my uncle John – I remember going down to Killester with my mam on her bike back when the marathon used to go through the Northside – pity it doesn't anymore! Then in the late nineties when I was a young teenager, the marathon used to finish in Smithfield; I came in with my mam and my auntie and about a mile from the finish I jumped in and ran with my da, probably in my Celtic jersey! I was more into soccer than running then, but if a match was cancelled, I'd do a run with my da. That's when I got into the running, really. I love that memory of running down the quays and then turning onto Smithfield and finishing with him.

Mick Clohisey, 2018 Irish National Marathon Champion and 6th finisher in 2:15.58

to put in the work and make the sacrifices and employers weren't willing to give people time off work to train. A lot of balance went out of people's lives at the time.

'Obviously, there were other factors as well, but the standard at elite level was awful for a few years. It is now almost back to where it was in the 1980s, though we are still waiting for an athlete who is capable of running 2.10 to come along. But there is decent depth there with eight to ten athletes breaking 2.20 each year. The difference in the 1980s was there were two or three runners doing around 2.12.'

The Marathon Mission programme, the brainchild of committee member Eugene Cop-

Above left: Paul Pollock on his way to winning the National Championship, 2012.

Above right: the lead Irish pack, l to r Brian Maher, Joe Sweeney, Sean Hehir and Colm Rooney, 2013.

pinger, played a key role in restoring the standards at elite level in male and female marathon running in Ireland. Coppinger and Aughney approached Hooper with the idea and in the early days AAI coaches Teresa McDaid and Jim Davis were involved.

By now the Dublin race was an internationally established marathon on the European circuit, but Aughney, who was an athlete first and foremost, didn't like the idea that no Irish runner was capable of challenging for a place on the podium. 'We were taking the event away from the Irish.'

Ireland had no representative in either the men's or women's marathon at the Atlanta, Sydney or Athens Olympics. 'I felt we had to do something,' said Aughney.

One of the key factors was finance. Finally, in 2008 the Dublin Marathon had spare cash. However, for legal reasons they were not allowed accumulate reserves over and above what they needed to finance the following year's race. They could, however, spend money improving standards at elite level.

In 2009 all interested parties gathered in the Spa Hotel in Lucan for the launch of a long-term initiative. In addition to specialised coaching, the prize structure of the race was changed to favour Irish athletes, who were also provided with a range of other benefits including funds to race and train abroad.

Instead of offering bonuses to the East African runners, Irish athletes would be compensated financially if they met certain targets in the Dublin Marathons.

At the height of the recession the marathon experienced its own wobble when it parted company with its sponsor the National Lottery prior to the 2012 race. 'We couldn't agree on

a financial package,' Jim Aughney told the *Irish Independent*.

But there was a silver lining for home-based athletes. Owning to budget constraints caused by the lack of a title sponsor no overseas elite runners were invited to compete in the 2013 race.

'The loss of the sponsor could have been catastrophic for the event. But for Irish athletes it turned into a positive,' recalls Sean Hehir.

He was convinced by his new coach Dick Hooper to switch to marathon running in 2010. Soon afterwards the Clare-born, Dublin-based primary school teacher joined the Dublin Marathon Mission programme.

'It was a brilliant initiative. Most of us on the programme were athletes with full-time jobs. Nobody else has given us the kind of support that Jim Aughney and his team did. They have gone above and beyond the call of duty for us.'

Hehir ran his debut marathon in Dublin in 2012. 'I was on cloud nine. I kept thinking that this marathon lark wasn't bad at all until I got near UCD. Then the wheels fell off fairly quickly and I discovered that it was a different sport.'

He held it together to finish thirteenth in 2:17.35 securing him a silver medal in the National Marathon Championship behind Paul Pollock and ahead of bronze medallist Barry Minnock, his best-friend, training partner and flatmate.

When an injury scuppered his plans to run in the Rotterdam Marathon in the spring of 2013 he focused all his energy on Dublin. 'I remember what Dick said to me: "Sean, you are

The support around the course in the Dublin Marathon helped so much – whenever I started to think 'Do I feel tired? or 'Why am I doing this?' the support just buoyed me up. I knew where my club mates would be around the course and sometimes I just concentrated on getting as far as them. I felt like I was running for them as much as for myself - I knew they'd be waiting for me, standing out there all day ready to cheer us all on – so I wanted to run well. I could hear them even before I saw them – and when I heard their voices, my feet just lifted!
Caroline Farrelly, who was on the winning National Marathon F50 Team 2018.

going to win it." For somebody who has always struggled with self-confidence this meant so much to me.'

It helped that much of the pre-marathon attention was on Joe Sweeney, who had finished an eye-catching fifth in the European Cross-Country Championships in 2011. Coached by Jerry Kiernan, he was making his marathon debut in Dublin.

Three weeks before the Dublin Marathon Hehir had a dream run in the Cardiff Half Marathon finishing eighth in a personal best time of sixty-five minutes and eleven seconds. 'I was thinking; this is fantastic all the pieces of the jigsaw are coming together. But nothing is ever plain sailing.'

Top: Maria McCambridge in Milltown, 2014.

Left: Sonia O'Sullivan, 2015.

Above: the wheelchair race in full swing, 2014.

Above: Leevale's Lizzie Lee finishes 3rd in the women's race and wins the national championship in 2018. 'At mile 22 a man with a strong Dublin accent shouted, "Stay with 'em Lizzie, you're doing Ireland proud" - he might as well have physically kicked me up the road such was the lift I got!'

An earache that had troubled him the previous week worsened the morning after the half. He tried ear drops ,but the infection became progressively worse. 'By Friday there was a foul smelling white pus oozing from my ear.'

On the advice of his doctor he went immediately to the Eye and Ear Hospital where his ear was drained and bandaged. He was released in the early hours of Saturday morning and made an appearance at the final training session and talk for the Marathon Mission team in the Phoenix Park later that day.

'I wore a big wooly hat during the session, which didn't go too well. I couldn't use the shower so I toweled down outside; changed my hat and went inside to listen to the talk from John Treacy, the last Irish winner of the Dublin Marathon. Other than Dick [Hooper] nobody else knew that I had an ear infection. I didn't want them knowing there was a chink in my armour.'

He was fully recovered by race day. As anticipated, the race boiled down to a duel between Hehir and Sweeney when the pacemaker Brian Maher dropped out after ten miles. Sweeney made his move at the halfway point, opening up a three hundred metre gap on Hehir, who held his nerve. He gradually whittled down the lead before overtaking Sweeney near UCD. 'Everything felt fantastic.'

But there was one final twist to come. Just as he turned left on to Merrion Road he collided with a cyclist. 'One second I was on top of the world and the next second it all came crashing down. Obviously the accident wasn't malicious or anything and the gentleman was just going about his business, but it was the last thing I needed.

'Suddenly my legs felt like jelly. As soon as I got going again I glanced over my shoulder and it seemed that Joe [Sweeney] was closing the gap. I vowed not to look back again. Thankfully, I got my rhythm back and held it together until the finish.

'It was an incredible feeling to win the race. Nothing can or will compare to it. I am a very proud Clare man, but Dublin is my home away from home. When I was growing up I would

never have believed it was possible for me to win this race.

'I know I'm not the kind of athlete that would win the Dublin Marathon if the elite runners were coming in from Kenya and elsewhere. I consider myself very fortunate that the stars were in line for me that day.'

His day of drama still wasn't over, though. 'I was doing some post-race interviews when Eugene Coppinger, one of the marathon organisers, whispered in my ear that my girlfriend, Olive, had fallen off her bicycle. She was on her way to St Vincent's Hospital in an ambulance.'

He contacted Olive when he returned to his hotel. She assured him that while she had sustained a broken collar bone there was no need for panic. Nothing would stop him from making his way to St Vincent's to be with his future wife.

Though Maria McCambridge was an experienced marathoner, victory in Dublin in 2013 was a validation of sorts. Three months earlier she had a frightening experience in the World Championship Marathon in Moscow when she collapsed in the early stages of the race from heat exhaustion. Despite checking herself out of a Moscow hospital, she had to undergo a battery of tests on her return to Dublin before being given the all-clear to run again. Like Hehir, she was being coached by Dick Hooper.

'Fitness-wise I wasn't in the greatest shape,' she recalls. Her win wasn't without drama either as she had to stop for a toilet break in Rathgar – this allowed Claire McCarthy-Gibbons to take the lead, which she held until the closing stages.

'It took me a while to get going again but I eventually regained the lead near the finish. It was the best feeling ever to win the race. I was on such a high and the crowds were magnificent.'

But the marathon is a cruel mistress. In 2014 McCambridge was in infinitely better shape. Now coached by Chris Jones, her preparations had gone particularly well and she was confident of running a 2:32 marathon and winning. Bad weather on the morning of the race forced her to change her strategy. After consulting with her coach she decided to stay in the lead pack and see how the race developed.

Eventually two Kenyans got away, but she caught them in Clonskeagh. 'They sat on me so I had to make a decision and I opted to sit in behind them. One of them surged ahead and I let her go. The position of the finish line was moved that year and I misjudged it. I was closing fast, but I just ran out of road.'

Esther Wanjiru-Macharia from Kenya won in 2:34.19 with McCambridge just four

seconds behind. 'I was gutted,' she acknowledged.

Even though Irish runners still haven't run world-class times in Dublin, the success of the mission programme was evident in last year's race. Cork's Lizzie Lee, of Leevale AC, was the star performer from an Irish perspective, finishing third in the women's race in 2:35.03, just seventy seconds behind the winner Mesera Dubiso. 'I cannot describe the feeling of crossing the line and securing my first National Marathon Title and a place on the podium. For me, it was the perfect day full of memories that will last a lifetime.

'The support throughout the race was by far and away the best support I ever received during a race, and the welcome at the finish line from Jim Aughney, who has supported my running for many years was incredible. My coach, Donie Walsh won the national marathon title in 1971, so to have him with Jim, my husband and my daughter Lucy at the finish line was extra special. I had been told that Dublin was an incredible marathon, but it needs to be experienced to truly understand how amazing it is,' said Lizzie.

The top Irish male finisher, Mick Clohisey, was sixth overall, two and a half minutes behind race winner Asefa Bekele. Four other Irish-based runners dipped under 2:20. 'It was a big deal to do Dublin, my home-town marathon. Firstly, there was the novelty of running

Below: 2018 National
Marathon Champions:
Caitriona Jennings
(Letterkenny AC, 2nd),
Lizzie Lee (Leevale AC,
1st) and Jill Hodgins
(Leevale AC, 3rd).

round familiar streets with so many people out supporting. And there was also the fact that my da had done it, as had my uncle and cousins while Dick [Hooper], my coach, had won it three times.

'Jim Aughney has always been a massive support, so I wanted to run Dublin for him too. And it was the national championship – the one national title I hadn't won. My race plan was to be as competitive as I could up front. I wanted to let them know I was there; I went in to race, to race at the front. Thankfully everything went to plan. It was great for my family and my wife Cróna, who were all out on the streets. Dublin just has that extra special feeling.'

'Having been through three Olympics in which we had no representative in the marathon it's great that we are back up to the level where we had six runners competing in the Rio Games,' says Hooper. Clohisey together with Kevin Seaward, Paul Pollock, Breege Connolly, Lizzie Lee and Fionnuala McCormack, ran in the Olympic Marathon in 2016. Hooper believes that Ireland can realistically challenge for a team medal in the marathon at future European championships.

Left: Olympian Pat Hooper, second from right, at a charity event launch for Bone Marrow for Leukaemia.

Below: Ray McCormack, secretary of the charity, Children's Leukaemia Research Project, who took up marathon running in his forties.

Chapter 11

Marathon for a Cause

Since its launch in 1980 the Dublin Marathon has been intrinsically linked with charitable causes, though it is virtually impossible to calculate precisely how much money has been raised over the last forty years. All the evidence suggests the figure runs into tens of millions of euro.

The value of a big-city marathon as a fund-raising event can be gauged from figures released by the organisers of the London Marathon who have estimated that since the race's launch in 1981 it has raised over £1billion for charity with the 2018 race raising £63.7m. Granted the Dublin race is on a much smaller scale. Nonetheless, the figure raised is likely to be tens of millions.

Seamus Kilcullen, who died suddenly in 2015 just a couple of weeks short of his seventy-seventh birthday, played a pioneering role in establishing the link between the Dublin Marathon and charities. He raised £78 through sponsorship for the Children's Leukaemia Research Project in the inaugural marathon in 1980. He completed every subsequent Dublin Marathon in a lifetime devoted to running and fundraising for worthy causes.

Ray McCormack, a work colleague of his in the then Institute for Industrial Research and Standards, got involved in the charity after a friend's daughter was diagnosed with leukaemia. They hit upon the idea of raising money through sponsoring a runner in the first Dublin Marathon.

'It was pretty basic,' recalls McCormack. 'We just had a foolscap sheet of paper which was passed around at work and people put their names on it.' From those humble beginnings the project snowballed. At its peak the CLRP had 250 runners raising money on its behalf in the Dublin Marathon.

McCormack progressed to be secretary of the CLRP and together with the treasurer Tommy Monahan organised the logistics on race day for their runners. 'We hired a room in

the basement of the Shelbourne Hotel where the runners could change into their race gear
and we provided refreshments for them afterwards.'

On the eve of one marathon McCormack got a phone call from two American lawyers who had raised 15,000 dollars. 'I thought it was a wind-up initially,' remembers Ray.
But there was a poignant background to the story. An Irishman adopted as an infant and
brought to America was visiting Ireland when he saw a letter in the *Evening Herald* from
the CLRP seeking runners to raise funds. He was touched by the idea, as a friend in the US
had a child who was recently diagnosed with leukaemia. On his return he penned a letter to
the *New York Times* similar to the one he had read in the *Evening Herald*.

On reading this the two lawyers decided to fund raise for the CLRP and run in the
Dublin Marathon. For years after their initial visit they continued to send an annual dona-
tion.

Having recruited hundreds of runners over the years, McCormack decided to become one
himself and in 1989 he made his Dublin Marathon debut at the age of forty-two. He ran
another thirty-six marathons in what proved to be a very successful career, winning championship medals with Raheny Shamrock AC in all the master age categories.

High-profile figures were also involved in raising funds through the Dublin Marathon. In

To the moon and back

Inspired by true love and a dream of a brighter future for their wonderful children, a group of parents founded the Clare Crusaders Children's Clinic, which provides free therapy and specialist treatment to over 450 children with special needs in County Clare. To finance this ambitious clinic, in 2005 Howard Flannery (RIP), Frank Cassidy and Ann Norton led the first small troupe of Clare Crusaders runners to the Dublin Marathon on a fundraising trip. In their distinctive bright orange t-shirts an army of Clare runners descend on Dublin every year since. Traditional pre-race inspiration is lavished on the runners from the steps of Buswell's Hotel and the purpose is clear – no matter what, 'Be proud of your achievement'. The success, pride and momentum that has gathered from the early days to the present is clear in the runners who have at this stage clocked up enough training and marathon miles between them to get to the 'moon and back'. With a steely determination the runners cover a tapestry of training routes in the vicinity of Ennis and surrounding countryside. The Dublin Marathon is undoubtedly 'home' to the Clare Crusaders runners, it is the pinnacle of the running year, where dreams become reality among friends who understand the meaning of it all.

Aine Quigney, Clare Crusaders

2005, Eamon Coghlan the former World 5,000m champion, led a team of nearly a thousand runners and raised close to a million euro for the Medical Research Centre at Our Lady's Hospital for Sick Children in Crumlin.

More recently, the remarkable story of the Dunleer-based Team Carrie illustrates the power of the marathon to mobilise communities to raise money, as well as being a catalyst for positive change in the lives of thousands of people.

David Carrie's life has revolved around athletics. From Dunleer in County Louth, he has a tangible link with the wider community through his work as a postman. His father was involved in Dunleer AC and David first tagged along with him when he was five years old.

Blissfully unaware of the bitter splits that bedevilled Irish athletics at the time, he simply wanted to run for Ireland. When he won his first All-Ireland title at the age of thirteen, he looked on target to fulfil his dream. Later, he realised the terrible dilemma he faced if he was to achieve his goal.

So long as he ran for Dunleer AC, he couldn't compete in major international events because the club was affiliated to the NACAI, which was not recognised by the governing body of world athletics.

At the age of twenty-one, he left Dunleer AC and linked up with another Louth club, Dúndealgan AC. He was now eligible for international duty because they were affiliated to BLE. 'My decision didn't go down well with some people. But I knew I had to make the change and I still trained with and remained friendly with the same group of lads.'

Left: Eamonn Coghlan running for Our Lady's
Hospital for Sick Children, Crumlin in 2004.

Below: David and Aileen Carrie, in a promotional
photograph for Team Carrie, showing the size of the
group they train in Dunleer.

The family that runs together: Team Kerr, David and Sandra Kerr with their son Aaron.

In 1989 he realised his dream of running in an Irish vest at the World Cross-Country Championships in Stavanger in Norway. Ten years later, he re-joined Dunleer AC after BLE and the NACAI agreed to dissolve their respective organisations and form Athletics Ireland. By then his marathon adventure had begun.

On 26 October 1986, Carrie and his friend, Ollie Devine, headed to the Oasis nightclub in Carrickmacross for a night out. They missed their bus home and walked for a couple of miles before grabbing a few hours' sleep in a hay barn. Then, fortified by two pints of milk they found outside a house – they left money for it on the doorstep – they started to jog their way home – a distance of sixteen miles. 'When we got to Drummin near Dunleer, Ollie turned to me and said: "Do you realise the Dublin Marathon is on today?" There and then we shook hands on a deal: we would run it the following year.'

Both were talented club runners specialising in 5km and 10km races, but they neglected to do any specialist training prior to the race other than one twenty-mile run. After ten miles of the 1987 Dublin Marathon, Carrie was sure he was going to win – provided he got the better of his training partner.

'We were in the lead group with Dick Hooper and the Klimes twins and we were saying to each other, "When are these feckers going to start racing?" We were used to running sub-five minute miles over the shorter distances. It felt like we were jogging as we were running

Drumshanbo AC at the Dublin Marathon 2018 – Doing it for Del:

Seventeen hardy souls from Drumshanbo AC took on the challenge of Dublin 2018 with a great sense of adventure and ambition. With eleven first timers this was a big deal for a small club, but we were not about to fail – thankfully over half were female so the twenty-week training schedule would definitely be adhered to! The training program was devoured and the WhatsApp group went into overdrive with messages of encouragement, positivity and the odd groan. A group meeting suggested a fundraising effort for cancer services in memory of our great friend Del who passed away in 2017 from this terrible disease. A GoFundMe page and sponsorship cards were in place in no time and our two thousand euro target was surpassed inside two weeks. And then came all the questions; 'What should I wear? What should I eat? Which gel? How much water? New runners? Anyone know a physio?'

Oh the fun we had. Suddenly we were experts … 'that's great pace'…'my VO2 max is up 2'… 'got a new HRM'. Garmin, Strava and WhatsApp shares continued to soar on the back of our efforts and the fundraising went nuts. Special vests were designed for the group and with taper week in sight it looked like all seventeen would make it to the start line … how many would make the finish line? Del inspired us, we wouldn't give up, we had trained hard, can't stop, keep going, do it for Del. Simple really, and of course all seventeen crossed the finish line. The tears, the laughs, the stories of the amazing Dublin support, we were in dreamland. The real story here was the incredible influence Del had on a small, ambitious running club and how we raised 10, 800 euro for cancer services. Friends for life. Did it for Del.

Drumshanbo AC acknowledges the efforts of Ailish, Collette, Collette, Cora, Debbie, Denise, Helen, Linda, Lisa, Tracey, Conal, Cyril, Damien, John, John, Neil and Paul.

Cyril McKeon, Drumshanbo AC

thirty seconds a mile slower.'

The pain began at the seventeen-mile mark. 'Ollie felt strong and pushed on and I was thinking not alone am I not going to win the marathon, I'm not even going to be the first Dunleer man home.'

Devine hit the wall at twenty miles. 'When I went past him I got a sudden burst of energy and I pushed on for a couple of miles before my legs buckled at twenty-three miles. I couldn't believe it. It was as if somebody turned off a light switch.'

He managed to make it to the finish, falling over the line in 2:29.53 to take twenty-eighth place. Devine stumbled in ten minutes later vowing he would never run a marathon again and he kept to his word. Carrie returned two years later. This time around he was more respectful of the distance; his preparations were more professional and he paced himself better, finishing twelfth in a personal best time of 2:27.17.

In 2008, Jim Aughney and Eugene Coppinger asked him to pace the three-hour group in the Dublin Marathon. In common with other big-city marathons, the organisers were recruiting experienced runners to run at a specific pace to help others achieve their goals.

'It was the first time I ran the Dublin Marathon when I wasn't either trying to win the

bloody thing or push myself to the limit. Instead I was helping others achieve their goal and I found the experience so rewarding.

'Once I stepped back from being a competitive athlete I realised that everybody was doing their best. It didn't matter whether they ran 2:30 or 4:30 they were all pursuing their specific goal, which was the most important thing.'

Overwhelmed by thank-you messages from those he paced, he was inspired to set up the Team Carrie marathon group in Dunleer.

His aversion to committees influenced his decision to establish Team Carrie as a one-man operation. But he did need the practical support of his wife, Aileen, who was a regular runner but had never competed in a marathon. Since then she has run every Dublin Marathon as have three other members of the group.

The project was launched on Gerry Kelly's *Late Lunch Show* on LMFM in April 2010. Eighteen people turned up for the first training session. 'I remember saying to Aileen, "We

Team James: James Casserly and his coach Mark Lacey. Twelve-year-old James has taken part in three Dublin Marathons so far and raised over a hundred thousand euro for Barretstown, who provide residential breaks for seriously ill children and their families in their base in County Kildare.

The assisted wheelchair and charity participants at the startline in 2016.

have a team.'"

He emphasised the collegiality of the group from day one. Training runs started at the same time. While runners were encouraged to run at their own pace, everybody waited until the last member had finished before having a cup of tea or coffee in the Dunleer AC clubhouse. He drew up a twenty-two-week training plan, which was individually tailored to meet the needs of beginners as well as experienced runners.

By the time the Dublin Marathon came around six months later, Team Carrie had thirty-eight starters. Apart from himself, they were all making their debut over the 26.2 mile distance. Everyone finished.

Paddy Dwyer, who owned a shoe shop in Drogheda, was very supportive to Carrie throughout his athletic career. In 2010 Dwyer was the chairman of the Gary Kelly Support Centre for Cancer in the town. 'I always remembered people who helped me so I asked the runners in the group to raise money for the centre.'

In the second year the group wore their own specially designed gear with their motto 'Carrying us across the line'. The project snowballed with 154 Team Carrie runners starting and finishing the 2014 Dublin Marathon.

'We had no grand plan, but it just got bigger and bigger and eventually I had to limit it to 130 runners because having 150 out on a training run on a Wednesday night was like having a race. So far 935 runners have completed the Dublin Marathon raising over €400,000 for various charities, but primarily for the Gary Kelly centre,' said Carrie, who was awarded the Lord Mayor's medal in 2012 for his contribution to the race.

He is a gifted raconteur, though when retelling Aesop's fable about the race between a hare and a tortoise he mistakenly referred to the latter as a turtle. He has never been allowed forget that gaffe. So much so that when documentary-maker Sarah McCann, who is a member of the group, made a film about Team Carrie she called it *Turtles and Hares*.

Their sense of fun is captured by the depiction of a pair of deer antlers on the running gear which commemorates the day team member Seamus Brett earned his sobriquet the 'Deer Hunter'. A musician and producer, Brett had no background in the sport, but was persuaded by Carrie to join. 'He wasn't taking no for an answer.'

His moment of notoriety came during the Race Series Half Marathon in the Phoenix Park. He was knocked over by a deer that strayed onto the course. Miraculously, he escaped unscathed – though his race number went missing. 'I actually didn't know what hit me until the runners alongside me told me that three deer had run into my path. I landed flat on my back and was able to pick myself up and finish the race.'

Carrie has a refreshing philosophy on marathons. 'It is a marvellous achievement to complete a marathon. Too many runners get hung-up about their time. Of course, runners need a goal and it is nice to have a target time. But I would rather see everybody finishing and going home with their medal than not finishing and going home with nothing.' Within the group he has never had a Did Not Finish.

His innovative side came to the fore again in 2013. He decided the group should travel together in a double-decker bus from Dunleer to Dublin on the morning of the marathon. A double-decker has seventy-eight seats so Carrie set himself a target of having a runner on every seat.

On the morning of the marathon, the double-decker was parked outside Pat's Gift shop in Dunleer. One curious onlooker asked him what all the fuss was about. Nonplussed when informed the passengers were *en route* to run the Dublin Marathon he remarked 'Well, we'll never see that happen again in Dunleer.' Carrie couldn't help himself and retorted. 'You're right there. I bet you €100 that next year we will need two double-deckers to bring the runners.'

Sure enough, two double-decker buses were needed to transport the 154 runners they had in the 2014 marathon. 'I'm driven like that. I love proving people wrong and he still owes me a hundred euro.'

At the start of the training programme, the group meet on a Wednesday night and also assemble on a Saturday or Sunday morning for a long run which takes them along country roads to Clogherhead Port. 'People living along the route now know when to expect us and they leave out drink, jellies and sweets for us. It's like a market at Port Beach on a Saturday morning because so much stuff is left there for us.'

The group now compete in the race series using these races to gauge whether they are ready to tackle the 26.2 monster. There is a social element as well with Team Carrie hosting a post-marathon function where all the finishers are presented with certificates and the total amount raised is announced.

'It is one of the best things I've ever done. I'd be long retired from marathon running, but for my involvement in Team Carrie. It's the sense of satisfaction you get from helping people that makes it so rewarding.

'We've had people with weight issues, depression and anxiety join the group. They all agree that running is the best medicine they ever had. We've had stories of people who were on medication for years going back to their doctors handing it back. They didn't need it any more having discovered running. The project has had a really positive impact on people's lives.'

Team Carrie's most accomplished runners Mark Hoey finished twelfth in 2:28.47 in 2013, while Priscilla Schultz ran 2:53 in 2016. 'The rest of the group look up to them and we've had members who couldn't break six hours when they started and now they are close to three hours,' said Carrie who at fifty-three still regularly churns out sub-three-hour marathons.

Carrie had a simple ambition when he started the project. 'I wanted people to get that sense of fulfilment when you hit the magic carpet and get across the finish line in a marathon. It's an incredibly euphoric feeling which can only be understood by experiencing it.'

Team Carrie is bringing the curtain down on the project after the 2019 marathon. 'I just want to go out on a high.' They have established the template for any community who wants to address their hidden fears and anxieties by competing in a marathon.

Every marathon throws up its share of poignant stories. 'Each year there are hundreds of these stories and some of them are particularly heart-breaking,' according to Jim Aughney. He has a particular affinity for the assisted wheelchair users, two of whom have been awarded the Lord Mayor's medal since its launch in 2011. It is presented annually to a participant for overcoming incredible odds or having an inspiring story fuelling their journey. Among big city marathons Dublin is unique in allowing assisted wheelchair users.

Team Kerr is a running team from County Down comprising David and Sandra Kerr and their son Aaron, who has cerebral palsy, epilepsy and a chromosome disorder. He was also born with chronic renal failure, which resulted in him receiving a kidney transplant at the age of thirteen. His dad was the donor. It was a perfect match and his progress has been excellent since.

Due to his medical condition, he is a full-time wheelchair user and has no means of verbal communication. Team Kerr's goal is to promote inclusion and encourage assisted runners to become participants in road races. Aaron was the recipient of the Lord Mayor's Medal in 2016 and he has completed the last four Dublin Marathons.

In 2017, Keith Russell's daughter Alanna was the youngest-ever competitor in the race when her dad pushed her around the course in a wheelchair. She was born with spastic quadriplegic cerebral palsy.

Despite her condition, she took on a new lease of life when out running with her father. They raised nearly €65,000 to buy a new minibus for the Meadows Respite Centre in Navan, which she attended. In December 2017, Alanna sadly passed away unexpectedly. Despite the tragedy Keith showed incredible courage by running the 2018 race in her memory and was presented with the Lord Mayor's Medal.

From the foolscap-paper record of the charity fundraisers of the early days to the online donations through Facebook, Everyday hero and the like today, the marathon has made an important contribution to the social fabric of Irish life over the last forty years.

Dublin Marathon 2014

Chapter 12

A Cast of Thousands

THE Dublin Marathon has a cast of thousands, but a staff of one. Carol McCabe has worked full-time on the event for more than twenty years with her role evolving to keep pace with technology, health and safety regulations and runners' expectations.

The marathon's first administrator Marion Kavanagh filled the role while holding down a full-time job with Bord Failte. She recruited McCabe, initially as a volunteer to tabulate results at the finish line.

'Back in those days we rounded up relatives and friends to help out on race day,' recalls Kavanagh, who joined the Marathon Race Committee in 1981 when she was twenty.

Her first job was to organise the provision of water stations on the course, which was done in co-operation with local residents associations and the Dublin Fire Brigade. Everything didn't always go to plan.

Marathon WARM UPS

PARTY TIME

The centrepiece of marathon weekend is undoubtedly the challenge of the 26.2 miles, but the Dublin Marathon is also renowned for the spirit of fun that surrounds the race. And there's no better way to savour that atmosphere than by joining in the Pasta Party and the Post-Race Party.

This year's **Pasta Party** will take place on Sunday night in the Supper Room at the Mansion House on Dawson Street at 8.00 p.m. Live music will accompany the pasta, provided by MacDougall's. Tickets will be available for £2.00 at Registration.

The **Post-Race Party** will be held on Monday night from 9.00 to 1.00 a.m. in the Royal Dublin Hotel on O'Connell Street (close to the Start/Finish area). By popular request, last year's band, 'Splash' will make a reappearance. Presentations will be made in various race categories. Entry free with race number.

● This year's goody bag is one of the best ever, with plenty of tasty snacks and drinks to keep you going before and after the race. Amongst the free items are: Two bars from Leaf, a Lucozade Sport drink, Dime Bar, packet of Fisherman's Friends, pack of Kellogg's cereal, bottle of Tipperary Water, voucher for Clerys Department Store and a race certificate.

● Refreshments available in the Finish Area are: High 5 drink, Cadbury's bar, Tipperary Water (natural).

● For the first time, the first competitor home from each of the 32 counties will receive a superb prize - a weekend away for two, plus a crystal trophy.

EMPLOYEE No. 1!

On Marathon Monday, Golden Pages most important employee will be Philip Green, from Malahide.

Neville Galloway, Marketing Director of Golden Pages, is pictured here with Philip, who will be running the marathon bearing race number 25 - to celebrate the 25th anniversary of Golden Pages Ltd.

Philip started running in 1981 when the running boom was in full swing and has completed 14 marathons to date. Of these, ten were run in Dublin, two in Manchester, one in Galway and one in Belfast.

Philip's PB to date is 3.26, which he ran in Manchester, but he is aiming for 3.15 in Monday's race.

HOLDING THE FORT

If you have had occasion to phone the marathon office for any reason, the chances are that the helpful voice at the other end of the line was that of Cecily McGuinness.

For the past five years Cecily, secretary of Clontarf Coasters, has worked in the Marathon office, dealing with every conceivable query and problem arising from the complex administration of the race.

"I first worked for the marathon in Millennium year, when the Coasters helped out with the water stations. Since then I have worked in the office, processing the entry forms, banking the money, answering the phones and anything else that needs doing.

"I love it, dealing with the public - even though it takes up to five months of the year. This year has been quite problem-free, so I hope I'll be kept on for another year!"

Pictured at the Golden Pages Marathon reception at the GPO, Henry Street, are (left to right): Eamonn Ryan, General Manager, An Post Mails (former Race Director of the Rathcoole Half Marathon), Alex Sweeney, City Manager Frank Feely and Neville Galloway, Marketing Director, Golden Pages.

'A few weeks before the race I would go out with members of the Fire Brigade to check whether the hydrants were working. One time we opened a hydrant on the Navan Road, the water gushed up into the air and we couldn't get it to stop. The local residents weren't too happy.'

The finances were always tight, but the committee knew how to improvise. Hiring a stand at the London Marathon expo was outside their budget one year. So a group travelled over and stood for hours at the entrance handing out promotional material for the Dublin Marathon.

'Committee meetings were lengthy affairs so we brought in our own batch bread, butter, ham and cheese and made sandwiches to fortify ourselves,' she recalls. While serving on the committee she never had an opportunity to run the race, but is set to run her third successive Dublin Marathon this year.

In the early years the marathon didn't have a dedicated phone line. Kavanagh took marathon related calls at work. Such was their volume around race time the Bord Fáilte switchboard became jammed more than once.

Likewise, Alex Sweeney would get calls at work in Player-Wills much to the annoyance of his supervisors. 'On one occasion the supervisor called me over and said, "There's a bloke on the phone for you claiming he is the effin' Lord Mayor". It turned out it *was* the Lord Mayor at the time, Michael Keating, who was attempting to broker an agreement between the BHAA and BLE.'

Cecily McGuinness, whose husband John was a member of the organising committee, worked in the marathon office for more than five years. In a Golden Pages newsletter published on the eve of the 1995 race she explained how she got involved.

'I first worked for the marathon in Millennium year, when the Clontarf Coasters helped out with the water stations. Since then I have worked in the office, processing the entry forms, banking the money, answering the phone and anything else that needs doing. I love it, dealing with the public – even

Lead bikes from Bray Wheelers Cycling Club.

Dublin Marathon 2014

I did my first marathon in 1982. When I joined Donore Harriers to improve my running I got involved as a course steward and then over the years was ask to join the committee, first as assistant course director and then, as the marathon grew, I took on the role of logistics manager.

I had an interest in photography and I thought my photos would showcase the marathon well. I also started getting photos and memorabilia in from other clubs and runners. So in 2009 we set up an exhibition at the Marathon Expo, and the archive grew from there. Dublin is the only marathon to have an archive like this. It's an amazing record of the marathon over the last four decades. I'm in

charge of the archive and I'm probably the only one who knows exactly where everything is in the archive room! I meet so many people at the Expo who love seeing all the photos, medals and t-shirts displayed; a lot of them go on to donate their own memorabilia and photos to the archive, so it keeps growing.

I have set up an email address, dublinmarathonarchive@gmail.com , for people to contact if they'd like to send in anything for the archive.
Dave Hudson, Keeper of the Dublin Marathon Archive

though it takes up five months of the year. This year has been quite problem-free, so I hope I'll be kept on for another year.'

Carol McCabe was immersed in sport long before her involvement in the Dublin Marathon. She dabbled in more than twenty different sports despite the advice of her father Mick McCabe, a former Dublin hurler, who wanted her to concentrate on one.

Later after befriending Kavanagh, she officiated at BHAA races and rose through the organisation before being elected Chairperson. She worked in secondary schools as a counsellor in personal development, which left her free during the summer months.

In the summer of 1997 when a temporary vacancy arose in the marathon office Jim Aughney asked McCabe would she be interested in the position. She accepted the offer and has been there since.

In 2012 I was lucky enough to be invited to pace the Dublin Marathon. I was one of the 4.15 crew and I loved every minute of it. I've paced every year since that first time in 2012. Since 2013 I've been one of the Sub 4 crew. Sub 4 is a big milestone and we always have a huge group to get around.

In 2015 my amazing husband Joe was one of the 4-hour crew I was pacing. Crossing the finish line that year was incredibly emotional for us both. Only nineteen months before he had suffered a cardiac arrest whilst out running. His life was saved by hands-on CPR and an on-site defibrillator thanks to the amazing Crusaders AC club mates and the Clanna Gael coach who were in Sean Moore Park that night. Pacing the marathon felt like we were drawing a line under that episode in our life. He's paced it with me every year since, and we enjoy it more and more every year!

Olwyn Dunne, marathon pacer

When she became the only full-time marathon employee every transaction was done on paper. 'We'd send out entry forms and then get them back together with cheques, postal orders and cash.' Making daily bank lodgements became part of her work routine.

The online entry system, which only accepted credit cards, brought the curtain down on the days of bank lodgements as well as the tedious task of inputting each individual entry. The only downside for her was the loss of personal contact with runners.

'Over the years I would have built up a relationship with runners who would be in contact every year explaining why they're running the event and how their training was going.'

She still has to field plenty of calls – mostly from disappointed runners who had either forgotten or overlooked the need to enter the race before the closing date. Overseas participants sometimes book accommodation and flights to Dublin, but overlook entering the race! These issues are more acute than ever since the marathon has become a sell-out event.

Don Cronin of Portmarnock AC receives his finisher's medal in 2018.

McCabe has collected a store of memories and developed friendships over the phone with dozens of runners over the years. One of her most poignant memories is seeing an American visitor burst into tears as she crossed the finish line. 'She was distraught and I went over to talk to her and take her away from the photographers.' It turned out her mother had run the race the previous year, but had died in the interim. Her daughter had decided to honour her memory by running in the marathon and scattering her ashes over the finish line.

There have been stories with happy endings too. In 2018, Shane Callaghan from Carlow proposed to his fiancée Marguerite Kinsella after they finished the race. He had set the plan in motion five months earlier when he entered both himself and Marguerite – who had never previously run a marathon. He waited patiently for Marguerite to cross the finish line and then went down on one knee to make his proposal and she accepted.

The Dublin Marathon now has an annual budget of close to €2m with KBC Bank taking over as the primary sponsor in 2019. The total prize fund excluding time bonuses is €108,250. Last year, Lizzie Lee collected €15,500 for her efforts while Mick Clohisey took

Dublin Marathon 2013

home €9,500. Overall Irish athletes were paid €29,125 in time bonuses in 2018.

Happy faces at the t-shirt distribution stand in 2013.

Unlike most big city marathons, the event does not have a full-time race director. Having previously worked full-time with eir, race director Jim Aughney now works a four-day week with them and devotes the rest of his time to his marathon duties. The outlay on salaries is miniscule. Aughney is paid for one day's work a week while the London Marathon has a full-time staff of nineteen.

The annual in-house review of the race is a robust affair. 'We are probably our own harshest critics. I guarantee you that if an outsider came to a review meeting they would walk out afterwards and say: "I'm never letting that crew organise anything ever again."

'We don't clap ourselves on the back because we have got things right. We concentrate on what didn't go so well. The event is so big with so many balls in the air, that it is very hard to keep them all up there all the time.'

Not every feature of the marathon has been a success. The Breakfast Run on the day before the race – which was specially geared for overseas runners – had to be cancelled because the volunteers who ran it were needed to work at the registration desk at the same time. The kids' race which featured for more than a decade was dropped as logistically it became unsafe to run it in the time frame available.

On the other hand the Marathon Expo, which takes place in the main hall in the RDS in Ballsbridge has become an integral part of the weekend marathon experience. Up to 140 volunteers work here at the expo handing out race numbers, t-shirts and goodie bags. In addition there are athletic themed trade stands, a photographic exhibition detailing the history of the race and talks on marathon running from well-known personalities involved

It was supposed to be a perfect ending to a perfect season. Run Dublin on the 2016 October bank holiday and then fly to New York and run the marathon there just six days later. But an injury in August put paid to all that and I was devastated. Then an opportunity to volunteer came along. A lot of the marathon volunteers are gathered from clubs and societies across Ireland and as a keen parkrunner I was asked to help out in the baggage area. The Dublin Marathon is famous for both its supporters and volunteers and having run the 26.2 miles twice before it was my opportunity to give back.

The baggage area is a more delicate operation than many realise. Military precision is required to take in, numerically sort and give back over 15,000 bags in what is essentially just a three-hour window. Two shifts of more than 120 volunteers are the first people the runners see and they're the last ones many runners will have contact with after the race. We don't just hand out bags, we offer an encouraging smile to the nervous first-timers or a consoling shoulder afterwards to anyone that needs one. It's getting the bag in double quick time to those not wanting to hang around or protect those too tired to move after their race. We take photographs of friends and make phone calls to match up loved ones. It was the best way to stay involved, My volunteer medal hangs on the wall with as much pride as any of my race medals.

Killian Byrne

Our story begins with four friends Aoife, Anto, Rosanne & me, Jay! When my dad passed away suddenly in February 2017 Aoife suggested we run a race that summer and so our training began. We'd never run a race before, and hadn't even considered a marathon. I'm convinced my grief led to a moment of insanity and the idea, 'Sure why not run a marathon?' Before we knew it we were signed up for the Dublin Marathon! The training required some serious negotiation, I had a two-year-old, and a second baby due to arrive a few weeks after the marathon, while Anto was moving house; it's fair to say our partners were super accommodating to our 'man time' out pounding the pavements. Many months and blisters and visits to physios later the big day was drawing near, but thanks to a tricky pregnancy my wife had been admitted to hospital eight weeks prior to her due date and was set to remain there until delivery. The night before the race a complication arose and she was told to prepare herself for the possibility of an emergency delivery in the coming hours. The next morning she told me there was a chance the baby might have to be delivered that day, and to carry on as planned and run, but make sure to have my phone on me and be ready to sprint to the Rotunda if needed.

Having raised over €1,500 for Bumbleance – the national children's ambulance service – the last thing any of us wanted was to disappoint those who had donated so generously. So with her blessing we agreed to run the race, sure I'd be back in the hospital in four hours, or so I thought! Aoife brought my daughter, Poppy, to Castleknock Village to cheer us on at the 12km mark and we ploughed through until the dreaded 30km mark when the cramps started to kick in. Somehow, with the knowledge my wife needed me by her side ASAP and with Anto's words of encouragement about my dad watching over me, we finished our first marathon! We raced across to the hospital – in my haste I forgot to bring a sandwich for my poor wife who had been following my progress on the race tracker on her phone. Thankfully my wingman Anto was on hand to race to the local M&S and ensure our marriage survived the ordeal of a marathon. No baby that day, that was a whole different marathon, and a story for another day!

Jason Cromwell

Top left: marathon pacers and volunteers.

Below: Race officials Pat Hooper (Raheny Shamrock AC) and Declan Poynton (Tallaght AC) await the leaders at the finish of the 2012 Dublin Marathon.

in the sport.

By far, the most poignant issue Aughney has had to contend with was the deaths of two runners during the race. In 2006 Michael Morgan, a teacher from County Louth, collapsed and died during the race. In 2013 twenty-seven-year-old Ricki Savage, a member of Thanet Roadrunners Athletic Club in England, collapsed on Merrion Square after finishing the race and died later in St Vincent's Hospital.

He was taking part in his first marathon with the aim of raising money for the British Heart Foundation. After his death, more than €3,000 was donated to the charity through his JustGiving page.

'When something like that happens it can really hit you hard and we have had two [fatalities] in the half marathon over the years as well. You ask yourself was there anything we could have done differently,' said Aughney. He was moved by the reaction of Ricki Savage's family when he attended his funeral in the UK. 'They couldn't believe that two members of the marathon committee had travelled over. They were bowled over.'

Realistically, there is no foolproof method to guarantee that fatalities will never happen

in a marathon. The medical facilities on site (provided by Festimed, who have won awards in the UK) are on a par with what's available in the emergency department of a large hospital. 'The medical side of the marathon has probably witnessed the biggest growth compared to any other area,' said Aughney.

Given its historical links with the station, it is ironic that the Dublin Marathon has had such a troubled relationship with RTE television. Granted, big-city marathons are notoriously expensive and technically difficult to broadcast live. But despite its position as the national TV station, RTE has rarely risen to the challenge.

Their first attempt to televise the race live in 1982 was panned by athletes and critics alike. Production facilities have improved beyond all recognition since. Cost is now the stumbling block.

The race was last covered live by RTE in 2011. Even then there was an element of black comedy involved. Three twin-engine helicopters were flown in from the UK to assist with the aerial coverage of the race. They were parked at Weston Airport near Leixlip, then in the

The wall of support at the Dublin Marathon Expo.

hands of NAMA. The marathon office was informed that the helicopters might be in danger of being seized by NAMA representatives and were flown immediately to Dublin Airport.

The London Marathon is reputedly paid one million pounds by the BBC for the television rights of the event. In contrast, the organising committee or the sponsors would have to foot the bill to secure live TV coverage of the Dublin Marathon. In 2011 it cost €400,000. 'The figure would probably be higher now and we simply don't have that kind of money to spend on TV coverage,' acknowledged Aughney.

Now the race is streamed live worldwide on Facebook and the reaction is very positive. The one downside of the absence of live TV coverage is that the Dublin Marathon is not eligible for the prestigious gold, silver and bronze awards presented annually by the Association of International Marathons and Distance Races.

In 2013, the Dublin Marathon was chosen as one of the flagships events in The Gathering, an ongoing government-backed project designed to attract the Irish diaspora to Ireland following the economic crash. As part of the initiative the Minister for the Diaspora, Jimmy Deenihan TD invited Sonia O'Sullivan to lead a team of emigrants in the 2015 race.

It turned out to be her last marathon and one of her most enjoyable athletic experiences.

Harry Gorman

Harry Gorman, who celebrates his 90th birthday in 2019, is the official starter of the Dublin Marathon. He has been involved in athletics for seven decades and is synonymous with the sport in his native city. A former National Marathon Champion, he has attended every summer Olympics since Mexico in 1968.

'I have run seven marathons in total, but it was the first time I could make sense of what I was doing in training. I had never really trained properly for any of the other marathons. I had a great run finishing in 3:03. I didn't try to get under three hours because if I had done, I would probably have injured myself.'

But what struck her most was how the event had changed since she first ran it in 2000. It was more a celebration of life than just another race.

'When I was growing up in Cobh there were only two people in the town who were known as marathon runners. Now a big crowd from the local club Ballymote-Cobh travel up to run in the Dublin Marathon.

'It's amazing to see all these people all over the country out training for a marathon. It's fantastic that it has becomes such a big event.'

Forty years after the foundation the 'Friendly Marathon' has become the Irish people's marathon.

Gardaí on duty at the Dublin Marathon.

The 2019 Dublin Marathon Committee: Front Row: Paul Moran, Joan McTernan, Dr Ui May Tan, Jean Carr, David Humphreys and Dave Hudson.
Back Row: Neil Kennedy, Eugene Coppinger, Paul Barnes, Jim Aughney, Michael McCartan and Gerry Carr.

Chapter 13

39 Not Out

Thirteen individuals; thirteen different stories – but all with the same epitaph. Meet the most famous Baker's Dozen in Irish sport – the thirteen runners, twelve men and one woman, who have completed all thirty-nine Dublin Marathons and will line up on the start line for the 2019 race.

Frank Behan, Michael Carolan, Seamus Cawley, Dónal de Buitléir, Seamus Dunne, Dominic Gallagher, Patrick Gowen, Billy Harpur, Mary Nolan Hickey, Martin Kelly, John McElhinney, Peadar Nugent and Donal Ward have travelled 13,293 miles on their way into the record books during the last four decades.

As they crossed the start line of the first Dublin Marathon shortly after noon on 27 October 1980 never in their wildest dreams did they imagine celebrating the ruby anniversary of the race by competing in it.

Seventy-nine year old Frank Behan is the eldest in the group. 'I can still lift my legs but I tell people not to time me with a stop-watch, bring a calendar instead.' His love of running blossomed when he competed in BHAA races alongside work colleagues from Unidare.

These events engendered a sense of comradeship and social interaction he had never previously experienced. He suggests it was fostered by the late Ciaran Looney, a founder member of the BHAA. 'He was a big man in every sense. He'd literally lift you off your feet in a bear hug at the end of races.' Moving up to the marathon was no big ordeal for Frank, who was a member of Clonliffe Harriers and had competed in their annual twenty-mile road race. But once he ran his first marathon he always preferred the longer distances.

Olympic gold medallist Ronnie Delany is a past pupil of the Catholic University School on Dublin's Lower Leeson Street. Ronnie's coach Jack Sweeney was teaching there when Martin Kelly was a student thirty years later. Interestingly, he didn't believe Martin's sporting future was in athletics 'I once did a schools cross-country race in UCD and in his best

Donegal accent Mr Sweeney told me that the next time there was a race on to bring my golf clubs instead.'

Kelly turned eighteen a couple of weeks before the marathon. He didn't tell his parents about his plan to run until his father mentioned seeing bunting being erected on the route a few days before the race. Despite their reservations, he comfortably finished his maiden Dublin Marathon in 3:35.54. Previously, he had never run more than ten miles.

Mary Nolan Hickey was an active member of St Benedict's AC in her native Arklow for twelve years when she saw an advertisement in the *RTE Guide* for the first Dublin City Marathon. Her late husband Tony Hickey also decided to have a crack at the new race.

Having being a sprinter, it took her body time to adjust to the demands of high mileage training. 'I did one long run from Tinahely to Arklow and it nearly killed me. I thought I'd never get home. At the start line I wondered what I was doing. The last six miles was like a war zone; runners were dropping like flies all around me and my calves cramped up, but I kept going.' She was the sixth woman in 3:39.04 and finished eleven minutes ahead of Tony.

Limerick native Seamus Cawley has been one of the fastest of the thirteen all-timers posting a career best of 2:35.44. At the age of twenty he dipped under three hours in his first

Dublin Marathon 2011

Marathon Men: Two familiar faces from the Irish running scene! At time of writing, wheelchair athlete Jerry Ford from Blarney had completed 451 marathons – and counting. He's done every Dublin Marathon since 1992 – apart from 1999, when he was away doing the Chicago Marathon. He's found a kindred spirit in marathon man, Dave Brady, from Rathcoole who's completed 840 marathons since he took up running in 1986. Dave says, 'Dublin is special to me as it was my first marathon. I have run it every year since 1986. The crowd support on the course is brilliant!'

attempt in 1980 despite having a hectic weekend.

Forty-eight hours before the race, he was best man at a wedding in Croom. The following day he ran in the Limerick Novice Cross-Country Championships and travelled to Dublin on the morning of the marathon. His coach Fr Liam Kelleher lent him his stopwatch. 'It was the first time I used a stopwatch in a race.'

Dubliner Tony Mangan who spent four years running around the world began and finished his remarkable 50,000km adventure by competing in the 2010 and 2014 Dublin Marathons. The day after completing the former, the Liberties native ran across Ireland as far as Dunquin in west Kerry, the most westerly point in Ireland. His world trip took him across North America, South America, Australasia, Asia and Europe before rounding it off by running in the 2014 Dublin Marathon.

Seamus Dunne has the fastest marathon time of the thirteen, having run a PB of 2:35.02 in Dublin in 1981. Shortly after running in the Community Games at the age of fourteen, Seamus linked up with Dunboyne AC. He was an experienced track and field and cross country runner by the time he ran in the first Dublin Marathon. The club boasted a number of experienced marathon runners including Eddie Reid and Tommy McDonald, a former three-times NACAI Marathon champion.

'I used to do the occasional long run with them. Dublin was my first marathon and it was a bit of a novelty. I never said to myself that I was going to run marathons. It happened more by accident. In those days most marathons would have less than a hundred runners, but here we had 1,500 in the field.'

Dunne discovered he had a talent for long distance events, running 3:07.28 on his debut before posting his personal best the following year.

Michael Carolan never raced until he lined up for the first Dublin Marathon. He had loosely followed Noel Carroll's training programme, which was published in the *RTE Guide*, but had missed a number of the scheduled long runs. He retains three vivid memories of his debut marathon.

'After about ten miles a fellow runner advised me to slow down. I didn't and how I regretted later not taking his advice. There was the euphoric atmosphere in Raheny where the large crowds reduced the roadway to a narrow chute and then the agony I felt as I tried to run up Nutley Lane.' But he still made it home safety in 3:30.21.

Another 'Lifer', Peadar Nugent finished sixteen seconds later. A member of Dunboyne AC, he had competed in sprinting and field events at NACAI track and field championships since the 1960s. He didn't take up road running until the foundation of the BHAA. He ran with a work colleague, Maurice McMorrow.

'We both felt the going tough from mile twenty-two to the finish, but we kept encouraging each other. The question of not finishing was never in the equation. We didn't talk about the "wall" as though it was a point where we couldn't continue. We'd have walked if the worst came about. There is a stubborn streak in both of us.

'In advance of the marathon the late Noel Carroll, in both print and broadcast, had advised runners to set a pace of one minute per mile slower than in training. Our training speed was approximately seven-minute miles. We followed his advice and aimed for a three and a half hour finish and unbelievably we were only a fraction outside that.'

Wexford native Billy Harpur was better prepared than most – he was logging seventy-five miles a week in training and had been a member of Sliabh Buidhe Rovers in Ferns since 1971. Unlike the others, he wasn't making his debut over the distance having run in the BLE National Marathon in 1979 and the Boston Marathon in 1980.

Donegal native Donal Ward was working in Dublin in the old Department of Posts and Telegraphs and joined a group of fellow workers including Eugene Coppinger and Mick Fennell – who later played key roles in organising the event – for lunchtime runs. 'Starting off I just wanted to lose a bit of weight.' He was persuaded by his colleagues to enter the race though his preparations were far from ideal.

He got little sleep on the night before the race as he was working in the sorting office in Sheriff Street in Dublin city centre. 'I knocked off a couple of hours early and got a few hours' sleep before the race started.'

In the 1970s, John McElhinney started doing long-distance mountain-walking events including the famous thirty-three-mile Lug Walk, which covers seventeen peaks from Bohernabreena in County Dublin to the Glen of Imaal in Wicklow. He also did walks in the Maamturk and Mourne Mountains – all at pace. He believes this background was the reason he completed the first Dublin Marathon in 3:44 with relatively little training.

Billy Harpur nears the finish of his eighteenth consecutive Dublin Marathon 1997.

The Belleek Plate

For years, any time Louis Hogan made a cup of coffee it reminded him of the Dublin City Marathon. A Belleek pottery plate which was presented to him by a race participant hung in his kitchen. It carried a simple inscription: 'To Louis Hogan for an idea whose time has come.'

Hogan had no idea who presented him with the plate other than that the person spoke with a Northern accent. Indeed, when he first saw the brown-papered parcel which contained the plate he feared it might be a parcel bomb. But after examining it the Gardaí reassured him that it was perfectly safe to open.

One day a gust of wind caught the plate and it smashed to the floor. 'I contacted Belleek Pottery to find out if I could get a replacement. Unfortunately they were unable to help me because I didn't have the serial number.'

The mystery donor of the plate can now be revealed. Eighty-two year old Pat O'Loughlin commissioned it as a token of appreciation to Hogan for coming up with the idea of the Dublin City Marathon.

A native of Belleek and a jeweller by profession, O'Loughlin ran a retail business in Castlederg, County Tyrone for decades. Marathon running was his hobby and he has ran in all but one of the Dublin Marathons – he was hospitalised for the 2016 race.

O'Loughlin was the last finisher in the 2018 Dublin Marathon crossing the line in nine hours and fifteen minutes after walking the course with his running partner Jenny McMenamin and her daughter Rachel. He has competed in more than seventy marathons raising in excess of €65,000 for research into Multiple Sclerosis.

Long before he took up marathon running he had achieved sporting fame having played on the only Fermanagh football team to win an All-Ireland title at adult level in 1959. He featured in the 'home' junior final win in Croke Park but missed the decider against London due to injury.

He had strong family and business connections with Belleek Pottery. 'I thought the idea of having a marathon run through the streets of Dublin was such a brilliant idea that I asked Belleek to make the plate for Louis Hogan as it was his idea.'

He plans to be back on the starting line for the 2019 marathon with his team of helpers, his son Ciaran, a back-up car with food and drink supplies and a replacement Belleek pottery plate for Louis Hogan.

Pat Gowen played Gaelic football, soccer and rugby and sometimes ran on the road to stay fit when he wasn't involved in team sport. So moving to the marathon at the age of thirty-two was a natural progression. He did a number of eighteen-mile runs before the race and was logging thirty-five to forty-miles a week in training. His marathon time was 3:22.

A member of the Irish Ramblers' Hiking Club, Dominic Gallagher had a residue of fitness built up before he tackled his first marathon. 'I had done some jogging for health reasons and as I didn't have a car I cycled everywhere. I was just "learning the trade" and I didn't do enough training for the first marathon.'

The last six miles were a struggle, but he still crossed the line in 3:06.29. Afterwards, he linked up with some friends from the Civil Service and formed a team that participated in numerous BHAA races. Though he subsequently joined Raheny Shamrock for a year he didn't continue with the club. 'I preferred a more casual approach to athletics. I didn't want running to dominate my life.'

Like race-winner Dick Hooper, John McElhinney lived in Raheny. After the 1980 marathon he followed Hooper's example and ran into work every day. He was a city centre-based chartered accountant. During the next quarter of a century he regularly clocked up seventy miles a week.

Running kept him stress free and helped him resolve work issues. 'The solution to professional problems would drop like the proverbial apple once every two or three weeks when I was jogging. When I'd announce at the morning tea break that I had a solution to a particular problem my

Mary Nolan Hickey completes her 39th Dublin Marathon in 2018.

colleagues' response was you got it "while you were out running".'

Dónal de Buitléir first heard about the marathon from Noel Carroll during their lunch-time runs in Trinity College. 'He was constantly talking about it, but in those days normal people didn't run marathons.' But such was Carroll's enthusiasm that de Buitléir decided to compete in the inaugural marathon and comfortably finished in 3.25. A native of Clonmel, he discovered he could complete marathons by running no more than forty miles a week in training. The formula worked as evident by his performance in the 1985 Dublin City Marathon in which he clocked a personal best time of 2:46.06.

Like most of the first timers, Michael Carolan decided to be more methodical in his approach in 1981. '*The RTE Guide* published a training plan devised by Dick Hooper. Armed with my vast experience I decided to follow the expert programme. I kept to it meticulously and probably because I went home for the summer to save the hay and turf, I miraculously escaped without injury.'

He cruised home in 2:51.59 which was indicative of the significant improvement the majority of the group showed within the space of a year. Martin Kelly ran a personal best of 2:47 in 1981 benefiting from being paced by a more experienced marathoner along the coast road in Clontarf. 'I didn't do a whole lot more training, but I was a bit more marathon-savvy and had read up a few books. As they say it's the pace not the distance that kills. I didn't feel great at the start so I took it easy.

'Then, as we were coming down Watermill Road towards the coast road I tucked in behind a guy who said: "Come on, young fella, if you stick with me we'll break 2.50" and I stayed with him for the next five miles.'

Billy Harpur has particularly fond memories of the 1981 race because he had done some training with the race winner Neil Cusack. Dominic Gallagher comfortably dipped under the three-hour barrier in 1981 and went on to run a career best time of 2:36.52 the following year. Running alongside his wife Una Quinlan in the Millennium Marathon in 1988 remains the outstanding memory of his odyssey through the streets of his native city.

Even though she had a young family and worked full-time Mary Nolan Hickey, then twenty-eight, was smitten by the adrenaline rush she experienced during endurance events. She was competitive as well, finishing fourth woman overall in 2:57.18 in her second Dublin Marathon. She used an adopted version of a training schedule devised by legendary New Zealand coach Arthur Lydiard.

In truth there were huge sacrifices involved. 'My husband had two jobs at the time and

Paddy Craddock was forty-five when he ran the inaugural Dublin City Marathon in 1980. He had already made an indelible contribution to the sporting and community life of Newtownpark and Blackrock in south Dublin. Over the next three decades he became synonymous with the event before finally hanging up his racing shoes at the age of seventy-five, having completed thirty consecutive Dublin Marathons.

He joined Blackrock AC in 1955 at the age of twenty, shortly after he married his wife Patricia. 'I played both Gaelic football and soccer during my teenage years. But with my new responsibilities I felt I couldn't afford to get injured. There was no such thing as sick pay in those days,' explained Paddy in an interview in the 1995 Dublin Marathon race programme.

Even though his work as a joiner meant he was away from home for twelve hours a day, he was a community activist long before the term was coined. He was involved in the local youth club, scout troop and, together with Fr Barney King and Fred Rogers, co-founded the female juvenile section of Blackrock AC in 1969. During the 1990s he served as Lord Mayor of Newtownpark for three consecutive years.

His three daughters Patricia, Eileen and Rosaleen all had successful athletic careers and he coached the Blackrock team of Catherine Rooney, Connie Kelly, Louise McGrillen and Patricia to a silver medal in the All-Ireland Cross-Country Championships in 1989.

The Dublin Marathon gave a generation of veteran athletes – including Paddy Craddock – a new impetus to their running careers. Paddy was forty-four when he made his marathon debut at the BLE National Marathon in 1978 finishing a creditable 33rd in 3:03.07. But it wasn't an enjoyable experience.

'I didn't have too much mileage clocked up in training. Then on the night before the race there was a seventy-fifth birthday party for my mother. One of my uncles got very merry and I had to drive him home. I suppose it was after two before I got to bed.

'I drove the next morning to Tullamore and ran the marathon. But I really suffered over the last two miles and at the finish line I collapsed into Patricia's [his daughter] arms.'

He was better prepared for his second marathon a year later in the 1979 National championships back in Tullamore posting a personal best time of 2:45.40.

Being competitive was second nature to him. On the day before the inaugural Dublin Marathon in 1980 he drove Patricia to Tinryland in County Carlow for a four-mile road race.

'When I got there I noticed there was just one guy who would beat me in the vets' section. So I ended up running the race and winning second prize in the vets.'

Twenty-four hours later he ran 2:52.22 in Dublin to claim 98th place – his best ever finish.

He ran a total of forty-six marathons including Boston and London and had an interesting experience when he ran in the Belfast Marathon in 1995.

'The problem was I gave up sweets and biscuits during Lent and then decided I would stay off them altogether. I really suffered in Belfast, but thankfully a women gave me a Mars bar at around the eighteen mile mark and that helped me get through.'

Back in 1995, the father of seven had one burning athletic ambition left – he wanted to win an international singlet. And he fulfilled that dream as well, representing the Republic of Ireland in the Masters' Home Countries Cross-Country International on eleven consecutive occasions.

Arguably his biggest challenge came in 2008 when two of his siblings, Jim and Tom, died suddenly within a month of each other just before the Dublin Marathon, but he still completed the race. Since 2012, his granddaughter Ciara MacNamara has run in every Dublin Marathon to commemorate his association with the event.

In May 2006, Paddy and his wife Patricia were presented with an 'Unsung Heroes' award by the Lord Mayor of Dublin Catherine Byrne and a year later their decades of volunteer service to the community was recognised by Dun Laoghaire Rathdown County Council. In 2007 he was voted Ireland's Fittest Grandparent.

Paddy Craddock died on June 20 2016, twenty-four hours after he had celebrated Father's Day with his family.

In October 2017 Olympians Ronnie Delany, Pat Hooper and Dick Hooper were special guests at a ceremony in Carysfort Park – where members of Blackrock AC train – where a commemorative bench was unveiled outside the clubhouse to mark the life and running career of Paddy Craddock.

I was working full-time as well. So most of my training runs were done very late at night and I got an awful lot of stick at the time. And when I raced, guys didn't like it when I beat them. But that's all changed now.'

On the forty-year marathon journey most of the group had to overcome obstacles of some nature to keep the consecutive streak alive. In 1989, Dominic Gallagher did the marathon on crutches after being seriously injured in a mountaineering accident the previous June. 'I ripped the left hip from its socket when I fell on Camara Hill in the Glen of Imaal in Wicklow. I was taken by Air Corps helicopter to Naas Hospital.

'I was determined not to miss the marathon. I investigated the possibility of using a wheelchair and the Irish Wheelchair Association were prepared to loan me a chair. But I later settled on the crutches,' recalled Gallagher, who got around in eight hours and 38 minutes.

In the mid-1980s Donal Ward relocated from Dublin to Lifford, County Donegal and was on the point of drawing a line under his marathon career until a work colleague Danny Byrnes persuaded him to train with him for the race. Nowadays, Ward dons a Glasgow Celtic FC hat in the race in honour of his other great sporting love. Now retired from An Post, he has perfected the art of race preparation and most of his training runs are no longer than five kilometres.

In 2006, Dónal de Buitléir was awarded an honorary doctorate by Dublin Institute of Technology in recognition of his contribution to the business world as both an economist and strategist. But despite working in senior positions in both the public and private sector every October he toed the line in the marathon. He has kept a meticulous diary of his training runs over the last forty years. 'They are a great study in how performances decline with age.' But one training run stands out: a twenty-miler from his home in Ballsbridge to the Vico Road in Dalkey and back. 'I did it after watching Eamon Coghlan win the 5,000m at the World Championships in Helsinki in 1983. I've always felt he never got enough credit for that performance.'

In 2010, Peadar Nugent walked the marathon as he was recovering from hip surgery, not caused by running but by being rear-ended in a car accident. Subsequently, he was diagnosed with osteoarthritis and advised by his GP to give up running. He is now content to walk the marathon. Last year, having celebrated his seventy-fifth birthday in June, he decided to ignore his doctor's advice and take part in the All-Ireland Masters' Track and Field championships in his category. 'It was one last hurrah. I collected bronze in the 100m,

silver in the 200m and gold in the 400m. I retired my spikes that evening a happy man.'

Seamus Dunne was still comfortably breaking three hours nearly twenty years on from his first Dublin Marathon. In the 1998 Dublin Marathon he did 2:51.02. He also won back -to-back silver medals in the NACAI Marathon championships in the early 1980s.

'Back in the early 1980s we had a good group of marathon runners in the club and everybody was competitive at the distance.'

The nearest he came to missing the marathon was in 2011 when he severed a tendon in his leg in a freak accident. By the time the plaster was removed the muscles in his leg had wasted away and time was running out. 'I didn't put on a shoe that year until August, but I made it.'

In 1988, Mary Nolan Hickey discovered she was pregnant a few months before the ninth Dublin Marathon. 'It was bad planning on my part,' she says with a rueful smile. 'The first thing I did was to count up the months until the marathon. I reckoned I would just about make it. I was six and a bit months pregnant on race day. I walked bits and ran bits and got through it.' The following January she gave birth to her third son Calvin, who weighed in at ten and a half pounds.

A born competitor, she has consistently broken new frontiers for women in the sport. In 1983, she competed in the first ever All-Ireland triathlon which was based around Greystones. She did the forty mile cycle on a borrowed bike wearing a hurling helmet. Later, she successfully completed the gruelling Marathon Des Sables, a six-day 156 mile ultra-marathon through the Sahara Desert in southern Morocco.

On New Year's Day 2018 she embarked on a 1,500 mile charity run around the coast of Ireland and raised €73,000 for the RNLI. She was grounded in Listowel when Storm Emma struck, but otherwise the run went without a hitch.

Running helped her to cope at difficult times in her life. In September 1984, her twenty-four-year-old brother died of cancer. Then in 1997 her eldest son Stewart died tragically at the age of twenty. In 2017, her ex-husband Tony Hickey – who had also run every Dublin Marathon – was diagnosed with three brain tumours.

She shelved her own racing ambitions and teamed up with Tony's friends, Tommy Godkin, Charles Fleming, Nigel Browne and Liam Murphy and pushed Tony around the course in a wheelchair to maintain his thirty-eight-year unbroken sequence. He passed away on 18 June 2018, in Rathdrum Hospital. Last year she completed the marathon despite breaking her shoulder in three places before the race.

'I started running in 1968 and little did I know how helpful it was going to be for me in my life. I remember talking to a psychologist once and he asked did I take any medication and I said that I run and his answer was that it was better than any drugs. It's great for mental health. When you're out running with a group you get chatting and it's a great stress-reliever. It should be prescribed,' suggested Mary in an interview with RTE's Peter

Sweeney in 2018.

Although none of the thirteen purposely set out to run every Dublin Marathon it gradually became a life habit as Kelly explains. 'It just became a fixture in my mind. There was a couple of years when I wouldn't have much training done and I would start questioning why I was doing it. But I knew that once October came around I'd want to run it.'

His first sporting love was golf and he didn't link up with an athletic club until he joined Raheny Shamrock AC in 2002. 'Being honest, I saw running clubs as being for elite runners and unfortunately that belief is probably still out there.'

In terms of his running career, joining the club was a seminal experience. He made life-long friends and discovered that wearing a Raheny singlet on marathon day earns instant recognition out on the course.

'The Dublin Marathon is synonymous with Raheny. The last few have been the most enjoyable because the crowds taking part and watching the race have grown so much. I'd hate to break the sequence now,' said Kelly, who is the youngest of the thirteen survivors.

Though Billy Kennedy only ran the inaugural Dublin Marathon – he deserves to be made an honourable member of the Baker's Dozen club having worked behind the scenes at every

marathon since 1981.

It all began by chance. From Ballyfermot, he moved to the northside of the city when he got married. He had a young family and his only recreational activity was playing rugby with a team from the Unidare factory in Finglas in Business Houses competitions.

One night he turned up to a rugby training session only to discover it had been cancelled. So he tagged along with a number of his team mates to a Business House road race in Mountjoy Square in Dublin city centre where he made his running debut.

The race ended in chaos after the front runners caught up with the back markers on the tight course and it was impossible to count the number of laps runners had completed. 'The presentation was called off and we ended up in the Abbey Mooney pub afterwards.'

Kennedy was hooked and ran the inaugural Dublin Marathon in 1980. Then, he made the fateful decision to represent Unidare at the next annual general meeting of the BHAA. There he was co-opted onto the committee and more importantly appointed the chief steward for the 1981 marathon. 'I had no idea what I was letting myself in for.'

For the next two marathons, he assisted results co-ordinator Ned Sweeney at the finish line. Even now, the mention of cones, chutes and streamers sends a shiver down his spine as he remembers the logistical nightmare of manually recording the finishing positions and times of the runners.

Following the departure of Frank Slevin and Brian Price in 1983, Kennedy was promoted to the role of Operations Director where, with Alex Sweeney and Marion Kavanagh, they effectively oversaw the running of the event for the next fourteen years.

In order for an event of this magnitude to run efficiently there are numerous unseen, and unfashionable jobs to be undertaken. Kennedy recalls spending hours filling traffic cones with sand and water on the day before the 1981 race. This was to ensure the cones, used to corral the runners into chutes after they crossed the finish line, would not topple over.

Later as Operations Director, one of his primary duties was to measure the course which was a time-consuming, laborious but highly technical job. It meant being out on the course before dawn and in the early days using an eighty-yard-long chain together with a measuring wheel to calculate the distance.

Liam O'Riain took over as Operations Director in 1987 with Kennedy as his assistant. Nowadays, on marathon day he is on duty in the finish area. Coincidentally, his son Neil will be the marathon's Operation Director in 2019 having recently taken over from O'Riain who has retired.

Remarkably, despite his four-decade long involvement in the Dublin Marathon, Kennedy found time to nurture his athletic career posting a personal best time of 2:43 in the Belfast Marathon in 1982. Later he switched to the gruelling Ironman Triathlon making his debut in Lanzarote when he was fifty.

On Sunday 27 October 2019 – which happens to be the same date as the first ever marathon in 1980 – Kennedy together with the thirteen lifers will be back to write another chapter in this remarkable tale.

Irish
RUNNER

1982

VOL 2. NO 8.
PRICE 75p (Irish Tax)

INSIDE:

○ Full Marathon
Reports.

○ Pictorial on Race.

● Gerry Kiernan — Feature

● Jim Dowling's Marathon

● New York Marathon

● Running with
Deirdre Nagle

DUBLIN CITY MARATHON
SOUVENIR
ISSUE

Marathon Winners 1980-2018

1980: Men's Winner: Dick Hooper (Ireland) 2:16.14. Women's Winner: Carey May (Ireland) 2:42.11. Wheelchair Winner: No Wheelchair participants

1981: Men's Winner: Neil Cusack (Ireland) 2:13.58; Women's Winner: Emily Dowling (Ireland) 2:48.22. Wheelchair Winner: Michael Cunningham (Ireland) 2:44.15

1982: Men's Winner: Jerry Kiernan (Ireland) 2:13.45. Women's Winner: Debbie Mueller (USA) 2:40.58. Wheelchair Winner: Gerry O'Rourke (Ireland) 2:32.44

1983: Men's Winner: Ronny Agten (Belgium) 2:14.19. Women's Winner: Mary Purcell (Ireland) 2:46.09. Wheelchair Winner: Gerry O'Rourke (Ireland) 2:24.52

1984: Men's Winner: Svend Erik Kristensen (Denmark) 2:18.25. Women's Winner: Ailish Smyth (Ireland) 2:47.30. Wheelchair Winner: Gerry O'Rourke (Ireland) 2:28.07

1985: Men's Winner: Dick Hooper (Ireland) 2:13.47. Women's Winner: Julia Gates (Great Britain) 2:41.27. Wheelchair Winner: Gerry O'Rourke (Ireland) 2:21.02

1986: Men's Winner: Dick Hooper (Ireland) 2:18.10. Women's Winner: Maureen Hurst (Great Britain) 2:46.27. Wheelchair Winner: Gerry O'Rourke (Ireland) 2:22.55

1987: Men's Winner: Pavel Klimes (Czechoslovakia) 2:14.21. Women's Winner: Carolyn Naisby (Great Britain) 2:42.08. Wheelchair Winner: Gerry O'Rourke (Ireland) 2:23.01

1988: Men's Winner: John Griffin (Ireland) 2:16.02. Women's Winner Moira O'Neill (Northern Ireland) 2:37.06. Wheelchair Winner: Andy Hynes (England) 2:12.57

1989: Men Winner: John Griffin (Ireland) 2:16.44. Women's Winner: Pauline Nolan (Ireland) 2:44.32. Wheelchair Winner: Chris Hallam (Wales) 2:04.50

1990: Men's Winner John Bolger (Ireland) 2:17.17. Women's Winner: Christine Kennedy (Ireland) 2:41.27. Wheelchair Winner: Gerry O'Rourke (Ireland) 2:05.58

1991: Men's Winner: Tommy Hughes (Ireland) 2:14.46. Women's Winner: Christine Kennedy (Ireland) 2:35.56. Wheelchair Winner: Chris Hallam (Wales) 1:53.20

1992: Men's Winner: Jerry Kiernan (Ireland) 2:17.19. Women's Winner: Karen Cornwall (Great Britain) 2:41.58 Wheelchair Winner: Chris Madden (England) 1:53.50

1993: Men's Winner: John Treacy (Ireland) 2:14.40. Women's Winner: Cathy Shum (Ireland) 2:38.14. Wheelchair Winner: Chris Hallam (Wales) 1:59.28

1994: Men's Winner: Steve Brace (Great Britain) 2:17.11. Women's Winner: Linda Rushmere (Great Britain) 2:40.17. Wheelchair Winner: Richie Powell (Wales) 2:11.27

1995: Men's Winner: Willian Musyoki (Kenya) 2:16.57. Women's Winner: Trudi Thomson (Great Britain) 2:38.23. Wheelchair Winner: Roy Guerin (Ireland) 2:05.47

1996: Men's Winner: Joseph Kahuga (Kenya) 2:17.42. Women's Winner: Cathy Shum (Ireland) 2:38.56. Wheelchair Winner: John Fulham (Ireland) 2:11.52

1997: Men's Winner: Joshua Kipkemboi (Kenya) 2:15.56. Women's Winner Carol Galea (Wales) 2:39.33. Wheelchair Winner: D Kavanagh (England) 2:00.16

1998: Men's Winner: Joshua Kipkemboi (Kenya) 2:20.0. Women's Winner: Teresa Duffy (Ireland) 2:39.56. Wheelchair Winner: John Fulham (Ireland) 2:04.10

1999: Men's Winner: John Mutai (Kenya) 2:15.18. Women's Winner Esther Kiplagat (Kenya) 2:34.24. Wheelchair Winner: John Fulham (Ireland) 1:59.06

2000: Men's Winner: Simon Pride (Great Britain) 2:18.49 Women's Winner Sonia O'Sullivan (Ireland) 2:35.42. Wheelchair Winner: Derek Connolly (Ireland) 2:57.12

2001: Men's Winner: Zacharia Mpolokeng (South Africa) 2:14.03. Debbie Robinson (Great Britain) 2:35.40. Wheelchair Winner: Kenny Herriott (Scotland) 2:55.0

2002: Men's Winner: Frederick Cherono (Kenya) 2:14.23. Lidiya Vasilevskaya (Russia) 2:32.58. Wheelchair Winner: Kenny Herriott (Scotland) 1:52.48

2003: Men's Winner: Onesmus Kilonzo (Kenya) 2:17.03. Women's Winner Ruth Kutol (Kenya) 2:27.22. Wheelchair Winner: Kenny Herriott (Scotland) 1:42.54

2004: Men's Winner: Lezan Kimutai (Kenya) 2:13.08. Women's Winner Yelena Burykina (Russia) 2:32.53. Wheelchair Winner: Emer Patten (Ireland) 3:27.47

2005: Men's Winner: Dmytro Osadchyy (Ukraine) 2:13.14. Women's Winner: Zinaida Semenova (Russia) 2:32.53. Wheelchair Winner: John Glynn (Ireland) 2:14.08

2006: Men's Winner: Aleksey Sokolov (Russia) 2:11.39. Women's Winner: Alina Ivanova (Russia)

2:29.49. Wheelchair Winner: Richie Powell (Wales) 1:56.35

2007: Men's Winner: Aleksey Sokolov (Russia) 2:09.07. Women's Winner: Alina Ivanova (Russia) 2:29.20. Wheelchair Winner: Richie Powell (Wales) 1:59.10

2008: Men's Winner: Andriy Naumov (Ukraine) 2:11.06. Women's Winner: Larisa Zyuzko (Russia) 2:29.35. Wheelchair Winner: Paul Hannan (Ireland) 2:22.56

2009: Men's Winner: Feyisa Lilesa (Ethiopia) 2:09.12. Women's Winner: Kateryna Stetsenko (Ukraine) 2:32.45. Wheelchair Winner: Richie Powell (Wales) 1:56.35

2010: Men's Winner: Moses Kangogo (Kenya) 2:08.58; Women's Winner: Tatyana Aryasova (Russia) 2:26.13 (course record). Wheelchair Winner: Paul Hannan (Ireland) 2:21.00

2011: Men's Winner: Geoffrey Ndungu (Kenya) 2:08.33 (course record); Women's Winner Helalia Johannes (Namibia) 2:30.35. Wheelchair Winner: Paul Hannan (Ireland) 2:13.58

2012: Men's Winner: Geoffrey Ndungu (Kenya) 2:11.09. Women's Winner: Magdalene Mukunza (Kenya) 2:30.46. Wheelchair Winner: Luke Jones (Wales) 2:03.39

2013: Men's Winner: Sean Hehir (Ireland) 2:18.19; Maria McCambridge (Ireland) 2:38.51. Wheelchair Winner: Paul Hannan (Ireland) 2:34:48

2014: Men's Winner: Eliud Tao (Kenya) 2:14.47. Women's Winner: Esther Macharia (Kenya) 2:34.15. Wheelchair Winner: Patrick Monahan (Ireland) 1:52.43

2015: Men's Winner: Alemu Gemechu (Ethiopia) 2:14.02. Women's Winner Nataliya Lehonkova (Ukraine) 2:31.09. Wheelchair Winner: Patrick Monahan (Ireland) 1:43.05

2016: Men's Winner: Dereje Debele (Ethiopia) 2:12.18. Women's Winner: Helalia Johannes (Namibia) 2:32.32. Wheelchair Winner: Patrick Monahan (Ireland)1:39.18

2017: Men's Winner: Bernard Rotich (Kenya) 2:15.53. Women's Winner: Nataliya Lehonkova (Ukraine) 2:28.58. Wheelchair Winner: Patrick Monahan (Ireland) 1:49.55

2018: Men's Winner: Asefa Bekele (Ethiopia) 2:13.24. Women's Winner Mesera Hussen Dubiso (Ethiopia) 2:33.49. Wheelchair Winner: Johnboy Smith (England) – 1:36.12 (course record)

Number of Finishers 1980-2018

Year	Finishers	Year	Finishers
1980	1,421	2008	9,342
1981	6,490	2009	12,416
1982	8,748	2010	10,778
1983	8,688	2011	11,686
1984	7,241	2012	12,217
1985	5,410	2013	12,357
1986	4,828	2014	12,296
1987	3,818	2015	12,938
1988	7,738	2016	16,762
1989	3,019	2017	16,104
1990	2,806	2018	16,251
1991	2,751		
1992	2,414		
1993	2,617		
1994	2,422		
1995	2,706		
1996	2,732		
1997	3,123		
1998	3,929		
1999	5,130		
2000	7,156		
2001	6,153		
2002	6,493		
2003	6,266		
2004	8,512		
2005	7,941		
2006	8,141		
2007	8,460		

PRODUCED BY "ATHLETIC PUBLICATIONS LTD", PUBLISHERS OF IRISH RUNNER MAGAZINE
P.O. BOX 1227, DUBLIN 8. Telephone: 538693 / 506477 / 506824.

Acknowledgements

My thanks to the many people who helped me to tell the remarkable story of the Dublin Marathon.

This book was the brainchild of Helen Carr from The O'Brien Press, who expertly edited the manuscript; commissioned the real life marathon experience stories and showed a level of enthusiasm for the project that reflected her personal interest in running.

Sincere thanks also to Emma Byrne for her eye-catching design which gives the book a unique perspective and to the other staff in O'Brien Press for their assistance.

It would not have been possible to tell the story of Ireland's greatest footrace without the help and co-operation of many people. From the outset, marathon director Jim Aughney was an enthusiastic supporter. In addition to a sit-down interview, he promptly answered numerous subsequent email queries.

Carol McCabe from the Dublin Marathon office provided invaluable assistance and allowed me access to the event's archive material, while Dave Hudson did likewise with his magnificent archive photographic collection.

Thanks is also due to many others who I interviewed either in person, over the phone or via email including Louis Hogan, Dick Hooper, Pat Hooper, Alex Sweeney, Brian Price, Frank Slevin, Billy Kennedy, Marion Kavanagh, Mary Butler, Carey May, Neil Cusack, Gerry O'Rourke, Sonia O'Sullivan, Conor Faughnan, Maria McCambridge, Lizzie Lee, Mick Clohisey, Sean Hehir, Frank Greally, Michael Carroll, Tommy McDonald, Enda Carroll, Nicola Carroll, Paddy Lennon, Lindie Naughton, Patricia Craddock-Smith, Niall Mathews, Paul Brady, John O'Shea, Kevin Sweeney, David Carrie, Aileen Carrie, Seamus Brett, Pat O'Loughlin, Ray McCormack, Ray Messitt, Vincent Browne, Tom Kelly, Martin Kelly, Maura Kelly, Mary Nolan Hickey, Frank Behan, Michael Carolan, Seamus Cawley, Dónal de Buitléir, Seamus Dunne, Dominic Gallagher, Patrick Gowen, Billy Harpur, John McElhinney, Peadar Nugent, Donal Ward, Ken Murray and Margaret McKeon-Boyle.

Thanks to everyone who responded so enthusiastically to The O'Brien Press's call-out for marathon stories, and submitted stories, photos and memories.

Thanks also to photographers Ray McManus, Dave Conachy, Owen Breslin, Eoin Fegan, Padraig Griffin, Brian Tansey, Fionnbarr Callanan and Dave Hudson and to the staff of Belleek Pottery and Pearse Street Library.

For their encouragement and help I wish to thank Brian Farrell, Editor of the *Sunday World*, Eamon Gibson, Sports Editor and David Courtney, Group Head of Sport Independent News and Media.

A word of appreciation to my sons, Paul and Colm, for their thoughtful suggestions and encouragement throughout the project. Finally, a special word of thanks to my wife Mary for the many hours she spent beside me on the couch knocking the first draft of the book into shape and proofreading the final version.

Credits

SEAN MCGOLDRICK is from Newtownmanor, County Leitrim and has worked as a journalist for more than forty years. He co-authored *Shooting from the Hip*, the autobiography of Kerry GAA legend Pat Spillane and *I Remember it Well*, the autobiography of the late broadcaster Jimmy Magee. In 2015 he wrote *Punching Above their Weight: The Irish Olympic Boxing Story*, which was shortlisted for the Bord Gáis Energy Irish Sports Book of the Year award.

His personal marathon journey began in 1982 when he ran in the Dublin Marathon and he has since participated in more than thirty marathons and ultra marathons.